Old-Time Camp Stoves

Camp Stoves AND Fireplaces

A. D. Taylor

With a New Preface by
Paul Dickson

Dover Publications, Inc.
Mineola, New York

Bibliographical Note

This Dover edition, first published in 2012, is an unabridged republication of *Camp Stoves and Fireplaces* as prepared by The Forest Service of the United States Department of Agriculture, and originally published by the US Government Printing Office, Washington DC, in 1937.

International Standard Book Number

ISBN-13: 978-0-486-49020-5
ISBN-10: 0-486-49020-3

Printed in Canada
49020303   2025
www.doverpublications.com

PREFACE TO THE DOVER EDITION

THIS delightfully illustrated primer on constructing outdoor stone fireplaces, barbecue pits, camp stoves, and campfire circles was originally published in 1937 for the Civilian Conservation Corps, or CCC, by the United States Forest Service.

The CCC was a New Deal program that operated from 1933 to 1942, providing work for unemployed, unmarried men, ages 17–23. Besides providing employment during the Great Depression, the goal of the program was to conserve and protect natural resources. By the time the program was discontinued, this Corps of young men had planted nearly 3 billion trees, constructed more than 800 parks, and upgraded most of the existing state parks. They built trails and roads in remote areas of the country and created golf courses and softball fields closer to urban areas.

The designs in this book are those which the CCC used to create these outdoor amenities in parks and along trails from coast to coast. Often created from rock found at or near the construction site, they were built for heavy use and long-term durability.

When I discovered the original version of this publication at a used book sale, I had an immediate sense of nostalgia when I realized that the high chimney stove on page 53 (Plate XII) is not unlike the one my father built in our backyard during the late 1940s. Other outdoor fireplaces in the book look like those that, while growing up, I often saw in parks at all levels—local, state and national. Come to think of it, so did my kids, because a large percentage of these CCC fireplaces or those based on their design were still standing while they grew up, and many are still standing today. According to a news report in 2011, custodians of one state park in West Virginia started a program to restore 20 original CCC fireplaces. The condition ranged from those that had been completely leveled to those whose condition was considered "not that bad."

The stoves and fireplaces in this book are timeless classics, and have a certain appeal in this age of expensive, propane-fueled stainless steel barbecue grills—and part of this appeal is that they were built to last a few generations rather than a few grilling seasons.

PAUL DICKSON

F O R E W O R D

THE national forests with their lakes, streams, mountain ranges, and mountain peaks, including an area more than five times as large as all New England, contain a large part of the natural outdoor recreational areas in the United States.

The Forest Service of the United States Department of Agriculture, charged with the custodianship of the national forests, considers these recreational possibilities as public resources, to be wisely used and carefully safeguarded. Because of the public demand for use of these recreational areas, the Forest Service, within the limits of the funds available and consistent with the primary purposes for which the national forests have been created, is doing everything possible to properly and adequately develop these recreational resources for public use.

The Civilian Conservation Corps, during the last 3 years, has made it possible to carry on an extensive program of work in the development of these recreational areas which otherwise would have been impossible or long delayed.

In order to protect the forests from fire, to provide sanitary safeguards, and to furnish suitable public conveniences, it has been necessary to designate thousands of campgrounds and picnic areas and to provide these areas with simple and adequate improvements.

On the great majority of campgrounds and picnic areas fires are essential for cooking, for campfires, and for warming fires. To fully protect the forest growth, on and surrounding these recreational areas, it is necessary that these fires be confined within camp stoves, fireplaces and campfire circles. The importance of appropriate design for these features has prompted the Forest Service to make a careful and extensive study of this subject in order to determine the types of camp stoves and fireplaces best adapted to use under varying conditions.

This subject is of growing significance because of the increasing importance of recreational activities not only in the national forests; but on all recreational areas throughout the United States in connection with which these facilities are essential.

Mr. A. D. Taylor, consulting landscape architect for the Forest Service, made a careful study of this problem during the summer and fall of 1935. He has condensed his findings into the following pages. As the author states, it is fully appreciated that this presentation of the subject cannot be considered as complete. The text and drawings represent an effort at this time to make available in clear and definite form, the most authoritative information compiled to date on the subject of camp stoves and fireplaces.

It is my hope that this publication will be of real value to forest officers and to the thousands of others responsible for the planning and construction of recreational improvements throughout the United States.

June 5, 1936.

F. A. Silcox

Chief, Forest Service.

P R E F A C E

THE tendency for an increasing number of people to procure relief from the physical and mental strain of earning a living, by seeking the atmosphere of nature in the national forests, parks, and in thousands of other similar areas, creates an important problem for those who are concerned in meeting the needs of recreation. The problem of providing campground and picnic-area facilities, especially camp stoves and fireplaces, is increasing proportionately. The importance of this problem is further emphasized by the fact that during the summer of 1935 the throng of campers and picnickers using only the national forests had increased to 8,000,000.

Because of the influx of people, especially into the national forests, the national parks, and the State and metropolitan parks, the use of the areas adapted especially for camping and picnicking would be impractical if facilities for cooking fires and for warming fires could not be confined to camp stoves and fireplaces, for the following reasons:

A. To reduce to a minimum, on wooded areas, the ever-present fire hazard.
B. To increase the convenience and the comfort of man's use of these forest areas.
C. To protect vegetation against unnecessary destruction.

The great majority of those who are seeking recreation in the forests not only desire, but require these facilities for their convenience and comfort. There is a small minority, however, who are strongly prejudiced against the introduction of any man-made facilities into the forests. These individuals have an innate love of nature "in the raw", and they fortunately are able to adjust themselves to the conditions of nature without the aid of these facilities which are normally a part of any important campground and picnic area. Those recreation areas which are provided with facilities to increase the comfort and convenience of the people who cannot readily adapt themselves to nature "in the raw", are the most popular. In the development of any of these features, it is not practical or necessary to attempt to provide the conveniences which one can have at home. It is necessary, however, to avoid too great inconvenience in the use of these facilities in order that those who are less hardy may reap the full enjoyment from their short stay rather than to expend their energy in adapting themselves to conditions to which they have not become accustomed.

There is adequate space, especially in the great primitive areas for the small minority who desire to "rough it", to procure full opportunity to live with nature as it has existed for centuries. The great majority, however, who are living their lives under conditions which do not in any way equip them, through experience or inclination, to provide sustenance and comfort without these facilities, should be equally able to enjoy themselves in their particular way.

It is to provide for the great majority that this bulletin has been prepared in the hope that those who use, and those who may have occasion to construct, camp stoves and fireplaces may be provided with information concerning the problems of location, design, construction and use of these facilities.

While campground and picnic area stoves and fireplaces have been in demand during a number of years in the well-developed recreation areas, it is apparent that comparatively limited study has been given to this problem, and there is a great lack of dependable information upon this subject. It is evident that no definite conclusions concerning the design and construction for the most appropriate and practical types of stoves and fireplaces to be installed on different areas have been reached. It is most important, because of the lack of information available to those who are seeking an answer to this problem, that this question be given further study in the light of the experience which has been gained through this greatly increased use during the past few years.

There appeared in a recent publication the following instructions or "specifications" for the construction of parts of a camp stove or fireplace:

Three iron pipes, preferably not over $1\frac{1}{4}$ inches in diameter should be run across the fireplace from side to side, etc.

The walls must be sufficiently thick so that they will not crumble. Wherever large flat rocks can be obtained, they should be used. The larger they are the better, within reasonable limits.

Is it any wonder that reliable information is desired, when agencies directing recreation activities are publishing information of this kind on the basis of which to design and construct camp stoves and fireplaces?

The conditions under which camp stoves and fireplaces are designed and constructed to meet the requirements of everyday use are widely varied and there can be no one type of either camp stove or fireplace which seems best to meet all requirements. It has been necessary, therefore, to include in this discussion all of the possible types which seem of practical value.

The author appreciates fully that no discussion of this subject at the present time can be considered as complete. This compilation represents an effort to bring together, within the covers of a single volume, the best information which is available at the present time, on the basis of which further study may continue.

This discussion applies primarily to the problems which are presented in the forest camps and picnic areas of the national forests. It may apply equally well to many other types of recreation areas and to thousands of recreational developments outside of the national forests.

In further explanation of any lack of completeness in the following text and illustrations, the author calls attention to the fact that no consideration is here given to the "sophisticated" and very architectural types of stoves and fireplaces, often of elaborate design, and frequently developed on private estates in close relationship with other architectural features.

The author deeply appreciates the generous cooperation of the representatives of the Forest Service, who have supplied a quantity of valuable information on the basis of which a number of these drawings have been compiled. He is also indebted to the officials of the Forest Service, who have made possible a first-hand study of the actual conditions on the ground in many parts of the national forests. To the many individuals outside of the Forest Service, from whom information has been procured during the past 4 or 5 years, while this study has been in progress, sincere thanks are extended.

For valuable assistance in the preparation of drawings and text, a word of sincere appreciation is due to Mr. H. Dercum, architect, of Cleveland, Ohio.

April 1936.

C O N T E N T S

LIST OF ILLUSTRATIONS

INTRODUCTION

THE campfire appeals to an instinct which is common to man and which can be traced back to antiquity. Fires will always be in demand by those who are seeking recreation in its different forms in the national forests and in other areas. They provide a means of creating warmth, of cooking, of lighting, of exchanging signals, and of fostering a community interest among those who are gathered in the campfire circle.

There are two types of areas in the national forests, and in other parks and forests, on which camp stoves and fireplaces are used. These areas are ordinarily designated as forest camp or campground (primarily for overnight camping use), and picnic area (primarily for daytime picnic use and seldom for overnight use). The term "forest camp" is generally applicable to any area in the national forests used for camping or picnicking or both. The term "picnic area" is generally applicable only to areas used for picnicking. On the other hand, the two areas have a distinct use, one for camping purposes and one for picnicking purposes; and in this bulletin the differentiation is made accordingly. Camp stoves and fireplaces are used on other areas in the national forest, known as special-use areas, which are particularly adapted for summer residences, and for summer hotel sites with overnight cabins.

The forest camp and forest picnic area are set aside for this particular type of recreation use. Many of the forest camps are occupied for periods extending from 1 or 2 days to periods extending over a number of weeks, while picnic areas are in most instances used for one and not more than two meals during any one trip. Both of these areas serve as centers of activity from which the occupants may take long or short trips for hiking, fishing, hunting, etc.

In the forest camp and in the picnic area, it is essential that cooking facilities be constructed in order to provide the conveniences so necessary for the majority of people. Those who use the forest camps, especially for camping use, require a more complete and convenient cooking unit than those who use the picnic areas.

The problems of convenience and adaptation to use, appearance, protection against the fire hazard, and maintenance must be discussed in any adequate consideration of this subject.

It is frequently observed in the national forests that forest camps and picnic areas are used so intensively and in such a manner that the forest ground-cover is unnecessarily destroyed. There is a "saturation point" beyond which these areas should not be intensively used. This point is in direct relation to the kind of vegetation and soil conditions which prevail upon any specific area and which must be considered in determining the type of development for any area.

Any man-made feature, however well designed, when introduced into the natural forest is an artificial note and an intrusion. It is granted that the ideal forest recreation area is one in which these features are absent. Unfortunately, man's use of these recreation areas, and nature's requirement that vegetation be protected, make certain facilities and regulations for their use entirely necessary. It is very essential that there be an intelligent conservation of the existing growth on all campgrounds and picnic areas if continued pleasure is to be derived from the use of these areas.

The attitude of the public toward the use and protection of the facilities which are provided in forest camps and picnic areas varies widely in different sections of the country. There are those individuals who seem intuitively to appreciate the effort which is made to increase their comfort and enjoyment by providing adequate and convenient facilities. On the other hand, there are those who are critical of these facilities, even though they evidence a certain respect for the use of these facilities. There is, however, another group (fortunately, in the minority) who are inclined to be careless and destructive. In some localities throughout

1

the country it becomes increasingly important on this account to so design and construct facilities for campgrounds and picnic areas that a minimum of damage from vandalism and careless use can occur.

Fireplaces are chiefly valuable because of the open blaze which provides heat and light so much desired by campers and picnickers. Camp stoves are primarily valuable for cooking purposes and are necessary where the fire hazard is great. Fireplaces should be designed so that they may be used with reasonable convenience for cooking purposes.

The amount of money available for the construction and subsequent maintenance of camp stoves and fireplaces is often an important factor in determining the type of unit. Some types of camp stoves and fireplaces require much more maintenance (replacing of parts, removal of ashes, and repairs) than do others of a simpler and more solid type of construction. The kind of labor available for constructing these units is sometimes an equally important factor. The type of unit which requires strict adherence to detailed plans in actual construction is not practical unless skilled labor is available. In any camp stove and fireplace, it is possible, without skilled labor, to misinterpret the intent of the plans to the extent that the completed feature may sometimes entirely lose the desired effect.

DEFINITIONS AND ADAPTATIONS
TO LOCATION AND USE

In THIS discussion the terms "camp stove" and "fireplace" are used to designate the two groups of units which are used for cooking, warming, and lighting purposes. These terms are not synonymous. There are times, however, when it is difficult to differentiate between a camp stove and a fireplace.

In some types which are easily convertible from a fireplace to a camp stove or a camp stove to a fireplace, the unit may be designated as one or the other. There is usually a difference between the camp stove and the fireplace. The stove is that unit which is used primarily for cooking purposes and has a definite solid plate for a cooking surface, and in which the draft is ordinarily controlled by a damper in the door or in the chimney, or both. The fireplace is that unit which is used primarily for light and warmth, and also for cooking. It is usually constructed with a grate over the firebox and sometimes with a removable plate; but no provision is made for the control of the draft by any door, or in the chimney. The fireplace is ordinarily used on the picnic area and seldom used on the camp area except in combination with a camp stove. On the other hand, the camp stove may be used on the picnic area as well as upon the camp areas. In all camp stoves and in all but the very simple types of fireplaces, the firebox is lined with fire-clay brick. Campfire circles (pl. XX) are a type of fireplace although they are usually constructed only for warmth and light.

In designing a unit for any camp ground or picnic area, the first step is to determine whether the maximum use of the unit will be in connection with picnic activities or in connection with campground activities. The person who comes to a campground usually remains during a period of days or weeks and he desires during this period to be provided with three meals a day and therefore to have reasonable convenience in the use of any cooking facilities. The camp stove is the unit which provides this kind of convenience. The picnicker is on the picnic area for a matter of hours only, and during this time it may be necessary to prepare not more than one meal. As a little inconvenience does not annoy him and in fact may add to the thrill of "roughing it" and of being "in the open" for this short period, he is quite willing to accept a certain amount of inconvenience.

In general it is more desirable that camp stoves and fireplaces be in fixed locations in order to avoid unnecessary destruction of natural vegetation and forest ground cover. If these units are moved indiscriminately over the recreation area, the natural vegetation is soon destroyed and the area loses much of its attractiveness.

In some picnic areas, especially those in close proximity to large centers of population the only practical solution in the use of the area is that of providing movable units (pl. I, fig. 6A) for cooking purposes. On such areas there may be an intensive use by hundreds of picnickers on one day and on another day the same intensive use may be concentrated upon some other area. In the meantime one of the areas is very little occupied. For occasions of such intensive use it is, therefore, essential to provide a considerable number of units of a movable type to meet the requirements of this intermittent intensive use.

TYPES OF STOVES AND FIREPLACES

THERE is a variety of types of camp stoves and fireplaces, ranging from the simple types shown in plate I, figures 1, 3, 4, 5, and 6, to the elaborate and massive types shown on plates XII and XIII. In addition, there are the patented types of (a) fixed, (b) movable, and (c) portable camp stoves, some of which are used as assembled after shipment from the source of supply, and others are used only after being assembled and encased in masonry. The simpler forms of fireplaces, similar to those shown in plate I, are excellently adapted for picnic use on the forest recreation areas and especially on open areas, because these simpler features are less conspicuous and more natural in appearance.

PATENTED STOVES
(With and Without Masonry Encasement)

These stoves have a wide use, especially in the more urban park areas. The type of portable stove shown in plate I, figure 2 (designed to burn gasoline), is popular, especially where adequate cooking facilities are not provided on campground and picnic areas. This portable stove is often used where only fireplaces are available and the camper desires a cleaner and easier method of preparing food. These stoves are easily carried in the automobile, and with a few minutes of preparation they are ready for use. In some areas a large percent of the campers use this portable stove.

There are two other groups of patented stoves, one of which is used without a masonry covering and the other is used with a masonry covering (pl. XIV). The patented stove which is designed for use without masonry is best suited for the more intensively used recreation areas under city conditions. This stove is not well adapted, from the standpoint of appropriate design, to the natural forest surroundings. On the other hand, the patented stove intended for use only when encased in well-designed stone masonry (pl. XIV) is an excellent stove for use on campgrounds.

CAMPFIRE CIRCLES AND OPEN FIREPLACES

Fires, either in campfire circles (pl. XX, figs. 3, 4, 5, and 6) or in open fireplaces (pls. II, III, and IV) are always in demand on recreation areas where the fire hazard is small. These features range from the small circle for individual camp units or individual picnic groups, and the large circles for community gatherings, to the well-designed open fireplaces. Their main value is not for cooking, except on campgrounds. It is for light and warmth. There is a certain element of simplicity and charm in the atmosphere created by a campfire circle or an open, simple fireplace. No extensive campground or picnic area is complete without them, and their absence can be justified only in locations where the fire hazard prohibits their use.

FIREPLACES WITH TOP GRATE OR TOP PLATE

On campgrounds and picnic areas which are entirely in the open, the camp stove and the fireplace should be as inconspicuous as it is practical to make it, because of the unattractive effect which is so often produced by any considerable number of more massive types of fireplaces on a single open area.

The most natural fireplace is one which is cut into the natural rock outcrop or ledge (pl. I, fig. 3), or a similar fireplace so constructed that it reproduces the effect of being cut from the natural ledge rock (pl. I, fig. 4). These fireplaces are most attractive in appearance and appropriate to the surroundings. Unless the natural rock outcrop happens to be of a kind which can withstand intense heat and water dousing, considerable damage will occur in practical use.

On some picnic areas, a simple form of standard grate with sheet-iron or stone sides (pl. I, figs. 6C and 6B) is adopted. This simple grate is supported on four legs which may be anchored firmly in the ground, if the fireplace is supposed to be in a fixed position, or the legs may be so set that the fireplace can be moved to other locations.

The stone masonry fireplace with both ends open (pl. II) is a simple and practical unit where the fire hazard is not great. Most open fireplaces are constructed with a definite back (pls. III, IV, and V). In all of these fireplaces, the cooking is done upon a grate or plate which covers a major portion of the firebox. The plate is sometimes used on fireplaces in preference to the grate because of the increased convenience of cooking, and to prevent smudging of utensils.

The fireplace of this type may have a top grate supplemented by a top plate, or a grate without any top plate. These two may be interchangeable. In some fireplaces there is a bottom grate; but this is an impractical feature, especially when the grate is only 4 or 5 inches above the hearth. The area under the bottom grate is soon filled with ashes and therefore becomes the same as a solid hearth. If the ashes are kept continuously cleaned away from the firebox, the cost of maintenance is abnormal and sometimes prohibitive.

In a few types of fireplaces, there is a single bar across the front of the firebox (pl. VI). When greater convenience in the use of these types of fireplaces is desired, the hearth is raised above the ground level in order to have the top of the grate at a more convenient elevation (pls. VII and X).

CAMP STOVES

The camp stove which is primarily for cooking purposes sometimes may be converted into a fireplace, as shown in plates X and XI. The camp stove with the top plate at an elevation of 26 to 30 inches is apt to be rather massive and for this reason these high units should be developed only on campgrounds where there is an opportunity to partially screen one unit from another unit.

There is a type of camp stove, known as the "oil drum" (pl. XXVI, fig. 10), and the "icebox" (pl. XXVI, figs. 9 and 11), which is very practical in actual use but very inappropriate for use in natural forest surroundings. There can be little justification, even from the standpoint of practical use, for introducing these types of stoves into the natural areas.

Camp stoves are sometimes constructed with a chimney notch (pl. VIII), or more frequently with a chimney which may be low (pl. X) or high (pl. XII). Camp stoves should be appropriately designed (so far as a fireplace or a camp stove can be so designed) to fit into the natural forest surroundings. High-chimney camp stoves should be confined to the heavily wooded areas where there is opportunity to develop the necessary screen of natural planting. There is little justification for the type of camp stove with the high chimney except in locations where the fire hazard is great and the high chimney with its spark arrester is necessary to provide the desired protection.

COMBINED STOVES AND FIREPLACES

It is sometimes desirable to use a combination warming and cooking unit as shown on plate XV. This combination structure is apt to be rather massive and it should be avoided wherever practical in favor of the construction of the convertible types of camp stove shown in plates VIII, IX, X, and XI. The combination stove and fireplace and the convertible camp stove are frequently used in connection with shelters (pl. XIX, figs. 1 and 5).

MULTIPLE STOVES

The multiple stove with the high chimney in the middle is a feature which should be avoided in forests, except where the congested use and kind of use on any area (especially the area of limited extent) makes the use of these units necessary. This type of stove may be constructed in units of 2, 3, or 4 (pls. XIII and III–A, figs. 7 and 8).

In general use, this stove in multiples of more than two (except where used within shelters) should be discouraged. The smaller type of stove in single units is much more practical and more easily controlled in actual use. A single stove unit permits a better distribution of use over the area and provides more family privacy. Its economy of construction, where multiple stoves are required, is one of the factors in its favor.

WARMING FIRES

On many campgrounds and picnic areas, the warming fire (pl. XX, fig. 1) for the use of community groups is a practical feature. These units are desirable in locations where the evenings are cool, and also in some of the mountain areas where the natural temperature of the water and air is somewhat below that which makes for comfort. They are often used in connection with swimming pools in the forest areas. There is much more reflected heat from these fires than from the campfire circle. They cannot be used with safety where the fire hazard is great.

COMBINED SHELTER AND FIREPLACE

Plate XIX shows types of shelters which are used either in connection with an outside fireplace, or in which a fireplace is constructed. The type known as the "Adirondak shelter" (pl. XIX, fig. 5) and the type known as the "Trailside shelter" (pl. XIX, fig. 3) are very popular, especially in areas where there are frequent and sudden rains and also where hikers use trails during the early spring and late fall.

There are also shelter buildings for use during inclement weather, in which campers may live and prepare their food or keep themselves warm.

BARBECUE PITS AND BARBECUE OVENS

Other types of camp stoves are the barbecue pit and barbecue oven. In some parts of the western regions of the national forests and in Puerto Rico, barbecue pits and ovens are frequently used. The purpose of these features is that of cooking an entire carcass or large portions of a carcass at one time, in order to serve large gatherings.

These units must be carefully designed, and constructed for practical use. They may be an interesting and a desirable feature on any large and intensively used picnic area. They are seldom constructed on campgrounds.

GENERAL DESIGN PROBLEMS

GENERAL CONSIDERATIONS

The areas used for campgrounds and for picnic areas range from the heavy timber with a very great fire hazard to the open mountain country of the east where oftentimes there is little or no hazard. In all of these areas the camp stove or fireplace should be designed, first, for practical use and, second, appropriate design in keeping with the natural forest surroundings. Sometimes it is imperative that the high chimney type (pl. XII) be used in order to avoid abnormal fire hazard. These massive stoves with high chimneys are strongly discouraged because of their unattractive appearance when placed in the natural forest landscape.

The opinion prevails that there is no such thing as an attractive and an appropriate camp stove or fireplace, especially when introduced into the natural forest. Many persons feel that such features are entirely artificial and must be accepted as a part of the practical solution of the recreation problem. They insist that the design should be for maximum utility, and no effort should be made to develop a design which might be appropriate to the natural forest surroundings, inasmuch as no design can overcome the artificial character of this feature. Careful study of this problem of design leads to the conclusion that very much more appropriate and attractive results can be produced if the camp stove or fireplace is designed to be appropriate to the surrounding natural forest landscape.

The general practice is that of adopting only one type of design for the units on an individual forest camp or picnic area. It seems to the author that such a procedure, literally followed, tends toward monotony and a lack of interest, which otherwise might be avoided through the adoption of more than one type of camp stove or fireplace on a single area—especially the larger areas. It seems advisable in some instances to introduce an occasional camp stove type together with the very definite fireplace type.

The design of any camp stove or fireplace should embody the elements of simplicity. It must be remembered that if the more elaborate types of designs are used, then the resulting details of construction will be proportionately more complicated and the relative expense and work of constructing these units will be increased. These units should be simple in design and primarily for utilitarian purposes.

In some instances, a variety of mass design can be produced by introducing a "batter" in the side walls to overcome a contrast between the horizontal ground level and the more or less vertical surface of the side walls. This result is seldom successfully accomplished in an effective way because the fireplace is normally low, and unless the "battering" of the side walls is exceedingly well done, the effect is not apt to be pleasing. There is always the danger of attempting to procure an informal effect by increasing the "batter" on the side wall, sometimes to the extent that the base of the stone work, especially on the higher types of camp stoves, causes inconvenience in the use of the stove because the person doing the cooking cannot get sufficiently close to the stove. No one standard of design is the most practical or the most desirable. There are a number of ways to design these units, both in mass proportion and in detail, and it is the variety of design which creates interest and avoids monotony.

In order to reduce the height of the camp stove or fireplace, especially the chimney type, and the type with the raised hearth, it is sometimes desirable to do some grading around the sides and back of the stove or fireplace unit as shown in plate VI and plate X. If there is available a location on a slight slope, the fireplace or stove may be set into the slope.

FACTORS WHICH AFFECT DESIGN AND METHODS OF CONSTRUCTION

There are important factors which directly affect the design and methods of construction for camp stoves and fireplaces.

The natural topography of the area will determine to some extent the type of design for camp stove or fireplace most appropriate to the area. On areas similar to the recreation areas of the national forests of northern New England, where the forest camp and picnic area is usually developed on open ground to take maximum advantage of the sun, the camp stove and fireplace must be as inconspicuous as it is practical to make this feature. On other areas, amongst the large timber of the northwest, it is entirely practical to adopt a type of design which is of larger scale and has much in common with the surrounding landscape.

If the topography of any specific recreation area is rugged and has considerable outcrop of rock, then the design of camp stove and fireplace should be governed accordingly, both as to the texture of the stonework and the kind of stone used for construction.

The number of camp stoves and fireplaces which should be constructed on any recreation area is determined by the intensity of use on any particular area and also by the type of vegetation which exists upon that area. If the recreation area is covered with a thick growth of trees under which considerable undergrowth and ground cover vegetation exists, the number of units is determined by the number of individual camp sites which it seems advisable to develop and yet preserve the necessary seclusion and privacy which is so essential to camp units. It is estimated that the average number of persons per camp stove will approximate five to seven during any one time. So far as practical, the units should be so separated that each family or each group may have adequate space and may have its own individual camp stove or fireplace. This is particularly true with reference to camp stoves. The mixed use of any individual unit by more than one group leads to confusion and results in unsatisfactory conditions. On campgrounds, it is usually necessary to provide one stove for each camp site, and on picnic areas to provide one fireplace for the occupants of each three cars.

Climatic conditions will govern to some extent the kind of construction. In areas where severe climatic conditions are experienced, and where there are extreme changes of temperature, the most thorough kind of construction should be adopted in order to prevent disintegration of the masonry and other damage by frost conditions.

If the recreation area has an established use which will continue for a considerable period, stoves and fireplaces should be of the most permanent types, which require a minimum of maintenance and which will endure through a number of years.

In some localities, there seems to be a prevailing inclination toward vandalism. In these locations, the picnickers, in particular, rather enjoy the satisfaction of seeing how much damage can be done to camp stoves, fireplaces, and picnic tables. Under such conditions, where these facilities are not used with consideration, an unusually strong and simple construction should be adopted. Whether or not vandalism prevails in any locality, the movable parts should be securely anchored, or attached with a chain, in order that these parts may be kept in proper relation to the camp stove and fireplace. Signs placed in a conspicuous location near the fireplace, and containing instructions as to the proper use of these facilities might avoid some of the damage which is now caused to camp stoves and fireplaces partly because of lack of this information.

In locations where the fire hazard is great and where it is necessary to douse the fire with water, a type of construction must be adopted which will withstand these extreme changes of temperature.

Larger and more massive types of camp units are adapted only to those locations where large timber prevails and where there is adequate opportunity to screen the individual camp sites from each other. An unfortunate effect will be produced in the general landscape composition if massive types of camp stoves and fireplaces are used in areas which are generally open and unprotected.

The question of fire hazard is also an important factor which makes it necessary to use a type of design and construction which produces the minimum danger of fire. In these locations of high fire hazard the use of the solid plate and the use of dampers and spark arresters in the chimneys may be essential.

The availability of different kinds of materials to be used in construction is an important factor in determining the type of stonework in any fireplace. The types of stone and the ease with which the stone may be cut to the desired shapes for any desired texture of stone masonry should be considered before the final design is adopted.

PRACTICAL USEFULNESS VERSUS APPROPRIATE DESIGN

The camp stove and the picnic fireplace must combine convenience of practical use with appropriateness of design. It is much more important in the camp stove than in the picnic area fireplace to provide a design which recognizes as an important requirement the convenience of everyday use. Many campers and picnickers will accept any type of design (even the "oil-drum" and the "ice-box" (pl. XXVI, figs. 9, 10, and 11)) however unattractive and inappropriate in appearance, so long as it is of practical use. Such sacrifice of design is unwarranted. The natural pleasing landscape deserves more consideration. There are ways in which to combine practical use and good design so that such encroachments may be avoided.

The height of the cooking surface of a camp stove should approximate from 15 to 24 inches. A height of 30 inches more nearly conforms to the height of the cooking surface in the kitchen range at home. Such a height is to be discouraged in the forests, because of the resulting massiveness of the camp stove.

With a hearth raised approximately 6 to 8 inches above the surrounding ground and with a depth of firebox approximating 8 to 10 inches the resulting height of the cooking surface (adding the thickness of the grate or plate) is approximately 15 to 18 inches above the ground level. Unless it is practicable to easily screen these cooking units from each other the higher cooking surfaces should be avoided, even though more convenient for everyday use by campers.

Campers and picnickers seek the forests and other areas for recreation and exercise; thus squatting beside the low (15 inches) fireplace, or bending over the slightly higher (18 to 24 inches) camp stove is one of the forms of physical exercise which is a part of the life out-of-doors. Convenience in camp life is a very relative term which to most recreation seekers may involve some expenditure of physical energy not enjoyed in the everyday life at home, and unfortunately to a very few it means the comforts and inactivity of home transferred to the natural landscape setting.

In the use of the camp stove it is essential to have convenient access to the cooking surface from the sides as well as from the front. For this reason, the height of the walls above the top of the cooking surface should be kept at a minimum. Sometimes it is advisable to raise the top of the wall above the cooking surface, in order to secure a more permanent type of construction. The fire-clay brick lining in the camp stove should extend to the underside of the top grate or plate, and this additional height of the side walls may be necessary in order to provide an anchor or suitable attachment for the bars or grate and to provide a cap which will properly protect the joint between the fire-clay brick and the surface of the stone wall. By keeping the top of the side walls level with the top of the plate or grate, it is possible to set pots and pans partly off the stove and partly on the wall to obtain varying degrees of heat (pls. III and V).

The thickness of the masonry walls, outside of the fire-clay brick, may approximate from 6 to 10 inches. Because of the height of the cooking surface, any greater thickness of the walls is likely to make the top of the stove not convenient to use.

It is often desirable to construct a stove or fireplace with an area of gravel or sandy loam (approximating 5 feet in width) entirely surrounding the front and sides of the unit. If this area is not provided, then the natural vegetation will be worn unnecessarily and the area will become dusty, inasmuch as it will be generally dry. If the natural soil is clay, then the convenience of using the fireplace will be very much reduced unless coarse sand or gravel is spread. If flagstone is available, a very few broken flagstones may be laid at the sides of the unit and immediately in front.

LOCATION ON CAMPGROUND OR PICNIC AREA

The actual site selected for the camp stove or fireplace should have natural surface drainage so that muddy conditions may be avoided during wet weather. The fireplace can sometimes be built into a slope which will produce a more natural effect, especially if some small amount of grading is done immediately around the unit (pls. VI, VII, and X).

Locations for stoves and fireplaces on forest camp and picnic areas should be selected to meet the following requirements:

A. Easy accessibility to tables, cooking utensils, and parking spurs (especially true in camp units) (pl. XXVII).

B. These units should not be nearer than 10 or 15 feet from trees, and should under no conditions be under any overhanging branches which might be injured by smoke or heat.

C. Adequate provision for a convenient working space around the cooking unit, and an adequate storage space for wood and other supplies close by the cooking unit.

D. The cooking unit should be so located that during the heat of the day the necessary shade may be procured, if the recreation area is in a section of the country where shade is desirable. In sections of the country where the sun is desirable, then the cooking unit should be located accordingly.

E. The cooking units should be so located that, under conditions of normal prevailing winds, the smoke, casual sparks or heat will not be blown into the tent or across the table. It should be noted that in some of the mountainous country the prevailing morning breeze is apt to be in a different direction from the prevailing evening breeze.

F. The unit should also be so located that in the higher altitudes and more open exposures where excessive wind may be expected at certain times of the year, the unit can be so protected that excessive draft will be avoided and the fuel consumption reduced accordingly.

Extreme precaution should be taken in order not to damage the roots of existing trees, especially the more shallow rooted types. Unless the fireplace is properly located, considerable damage may be done to the roots of existing trees by the concentrated lye which leaches from the ashes. Injury may be done to the roots by the intense traffic over any root areas. It is very desirable that the unit be located so that the prevailing wind will not carry the intense heat into the foliage.

On some campgrounds in parts of the country similar to those of northern Montana and northern New England (in the White Mountains) the necessity for sunlight is equally as important as for shade in the southerly areas which experience intense heat. Sunlight is important in some areas in the early morning and, therefore, the ideal location for the camp stove and table is one which receives sunlight during the morning hours.

On recreation areas which are close to the lake shore, the stove or fireplace should be so oriented that the opening will be toward the lake, from which direction the prevailing breeze usually comes. In locations protected from the wind at all times, such as in heavy timber, the question of orientation is not important. This is likewise the case with camp stoves of the high-chimney type, where the chimney provides the natural draft.

In the fireplace type, especially those types which have a chimney-notch effect, and in those types without a chimney but with one end closed, it is most essential that the opening to the firebox be directed toward the prevailing wind. A very careful study should be made of the prevailing wind and the extent to which it is constant in any one direction during any definite time of the year, in order to orient the fireplace accordingly.

On most campgrounds, the automobile is the family larder, and for this reason there is considerable traffic between the camp stove and the automobile. The distance between the camp stove and the parking spur should, therefore, not be so great that inconvenience will be experienced in going from the stove to the car (pl. XXVII).

The cooking unit should not be located where there is excessive wind exposure, and this is particularly true in areas which have a considerable fire hazard.

On some picnic areas designed for group picnics, it may be desirable to have the stove or fireplace in multiple units as shown on plates XIII and III–A. The multiple units may be located at one or at both ends of the picnic area.

FIRE HAZARD

Whenever one seeks the forest as a source of recreation and has occasion to build a fire for cooking or for warming purposes, he immediately creates a fire hazard. This fire hazard may be very small upon the more open areas where the types of vegetation are not dense or of a kind not readily inflammable. On other areas the fire hazard may be very great, especially in the large types of evergreen timber and in arid sections where extremely dry weather prevails during the hot summer months, which include the period of heaviest recreational use. In the forest areas where duff and humus are on the ground in any amount, it is very important that sand or gravel be spread over the surface of the ground to a distance of at least 5 feet from the fireplace at the front and on the sides. This duff is highly inflammable and in general it should be entirely removed or else well covered with sand or gravel. In some instances an area approximating 6 to 8 feet in width and of equal length is sometimes paved with flagging immediately in front of camp stove or fireplace. An area of paving of this size is not necessary and usually detracts very much from the appearance of the camp stove or fireplace.

There are a number of methods which are adopted for controlling the fire hazard. Among the more effective of these methods are the following:

A. Use of water or earth to extinguish fires before leaving them. (Earth is preferred where fireplace is not lined with fire-clay brick.)
B. Construction of chimneys with dampers and spark arresters.
C. Construction of fire lane around the recreation area.
D. Use of a type of fuel which produces a minimum quantity of sparks.
E. Use of plates instead of grates for fireplaces.

Since fire is the worst enemy of the forest, it is important that all stoves and fireplaces be located and designed to create a minimum fire hazard.

FUEL PROBLEMS

When the campground or picnic area is located where there is an ample supply of fuel, the fuel problem is not an important factor. Difficulty is encountered where the supply of wood for fuel is limited. In some of the suburban, municipal, and metropolitan park areas near large centers of population, the fuel problem is very serious. In such areas, it is almost necessary to confine the use of fuel to charcoal.

It is advisable, whether or not fuel is scarce, to have some method of controlling the use of fuel and, especially, of discouraging its excessive use. On some campgrounds and picnic areas, the occupants cut their own wood from a designated area, and the trees which may be removed are definitely marked or designated. In hardwood forests, this procedure is not practical because the green wood is difficult to burn.

Wherever a supply of wood for stove and fireplace use is placed in piles near the camp stove or fireplace, and the occupants are allowed to use it freely and without charge, there is apt to be a great waste of fuel and an increased cost of maintenance. On the other hand, if suitable fuel is stored in a stock pile within a reasonable distance of any group of fireplaces or stoves, the occupants of the area will be less inclined to waste wood, because of the additional labor required to carry the extra wood from the stock pile to the fireplace. In general, wood is more apt to be wasted on picnic areas than upon campgrounds.

The most effective procedure for controlling the consumption of fuel is to authorize someone to maintain, for the benefit of any intensively used campground or picnic area, a "wood yard" from which wood may be purchased. Through such a concession the campers and picnickers are not inclined to waste fuel, and the maintenance cost otherwise incurred for providing fuel is avoided. In some recreation areas wood is supplied in bundles and a small charge is made for each bundle as it is taken from the "wood yard."

On intensively used campgrounds and picnic areas the Forest Service will probably find it advisable to furnish firewood through a concessionaire for a service charge sufficient to cover this item and other items of service essential for the proper administration of the area.

In densely wooded areas where fireplaces are situated in such locations that the sparks from the burning wood may set fire to the surrounding trees, the picnickers should be requested to use charcoal, which they bring or may buy on the site.

DISCUSSION OF DETAILED DESIGN

FOUNDATIONS

Fireplaces which are constructed of loose boulders (pl. I, fig. 1) require no foundation. The lower stones should be set into the ground approximately one-half of their depth.

All stoves and fireplaces of masonry construction should set upon a concrete or a masonry foundation.

The foundation may be of two kinds:

(a) A reenforced concrete slab which does not extend below the frost depth (pls. II, IV, and VIII).

(b) A concrete or masonry foundation which extends below the frost depth (pls. XI and XII).

In locations where it is not practical to construct concrete foundations, the grate shown in plate III may be anchored with a "log deadman" as shown in figure 6.

The concrete slab must be properly reenforced with wire mesh or bars, in order to prevent any rupture from frost action. The foundation which extends below the frost line need not be reenforced, and may be constructed of stone, brick, concrete, or cement block, or any similar material which is available in the locality.

In constructing the foundation, a pit of the proper dimensions is excavated. The reenforced concrete "floating pad" should rest upon the natural subsoil. If any fill is necessary on which to construct the reenforced concrete pad, it should be limited to a few inches (otherwise another location should be selected), and this fill should preferably consist of masonry, although it may be laid "dry" if thoroughly compacted.

For the foundation which extends below frost depth, the bottom of the pit is filled with a mixture of concrete into which "spalls" may be thrown. The material is thoroughly tamped and the concrete constructed upon it.

The concrete mixture should be as follows:

(a) Where screened aggregate is used, the mixture should be one part cement, two parts sand, and four parts of coarse aggregate, graded to a size of approximately 1 inch.

(b) Where unscreened aggregate is used, the mixture should be one part cement, and six parts of pregraded gravel with a maximum size of gravel passing a 1½-inch screen.

If the fireplace is generally low, and there is no excessive weight at one end, which might cause the structure to settle unequally, a reenforced concrete "floating pad" is sufficient for all normal requirements (pls. II and IV). The average height of the low fireplace including this proposed foundation is approximately 24 to 30 inches. The resulting weight per square foot approximates 480 pounds. Average clay soil is capable of supporting approximately 1 ton per square foot, or four times this load. Inasmuch as the average site chosen for a fireplace is on the firmer soils, the normal weight is far below that which the soil is capable of supporting and therefore, the question of foundations in the majority of these fireplaces, even where extreme temperatures are experienced, is one of providing a footing which is properly reenforced near the upper surface (pl. IV, fig. 4) to allow for the heaving and settling of the fireplace as a unit.

In most of the larger camp stoves with a chimney, where excessive weight occurs at the chimney end, the foundation wall should extend below the frost line (pl. XI).

FIREBOX

The size of the firebox has a direct bearing on fuel consumption. In areas where fuel is scarce and charcoal is used, its size should be kept to the minimum dimensions (height 6 to 7 inches, length 18 inches, width 12 to 14 inches). It is also desirable when charcoal is used as a fuel, to so design the firebox that there is a small opening in the bottom of the firebox through which the necessary draft may be created, to cause the necessary combustion in charcoal. The firebox in the camp stove (used for cooking only) requires less width than the firebox in the fireplace (used also as a warming feature). The cooking surface should be of sufficient area (average area approximates $2\frac{1}{2}$ square feet) to accommodate at least a frying pan and a coffee pot. The area may be increased, as hereafter explained, if more cooking surface is required.

The size of the firebox is to some extent determined by the amount of surface which is desired for cooking purposes. In the larger unit, the dimensions will approximate the following: Height 8 to 10 inches, length 20 to 30 inches, and width 12 to 18 inches. The height is normally from 8 to 10 inches, inasmuch as the best cooking fire comes from the glowing coals rather than from a high flaming fire.

In order to procure increased cooking and warming surface and at the same time preserve the minimum dimensions of the firebox, a type of design may be adopted as shown on plate XIII, figure 3. The open area between the firebox and the flue virtually becomes a part of the flue, although it is covered with a solid plate, the surface of which is sufficiently hot for cooking.

The open end of the firebox should face the prevailing wind. The shape of the firebox is normally rectangular. Sides splayed to the front are of some advantage in the case of a warming fire; but they add to the difficulty of procuring and installing the grates, plates, and lining.

In all stoves and fireplaces the firebox should be so constructed that there is a slight slope from the back of the hearth to the front of the hearth, in order that any water which accumulates on the hearth will immediately drain out of the firebox.

Because of the fact that the ordinary kind of stone available for camp stoves and fireplaces is not resistant to sudden extremes of heat and cold without undue damage, the best practice is to line the firebox with fire-clay brick in order to protect the stonework against direct exposure to these extremes. In some instances, a lining of 10-gage sheet iron, made to conform to the measurements of the proposed firebox, and with a grating attached, is used in place of firebrick. These combined grates and sheet-iron sides can be manufactured at small cost, and where the cost of procuring fire brick is abnormal, this type of lining is a practical answer to the problem of protecting the stone-masonry

sides against injury from direct exposure to the fire.

Sometimes it has seemed desirable to construct a precast firebox of reinforced concrete, so that the firebox may be set into a space surrounded by stone masonry walls which forms the shell of the camp stove. The theory being that if the firebox is damaged by heat it can be removed easily and replaced by another firebox. This procedure does not seem to be a logical procedure for the reason that a firebox of a much more permanent character can be constructed of fire-clay brick as a permanent part of a camp stove. Concrete thus exposed to intense heat will undoubtedly suffer definite damage in a very short time.

Ordinary brick is sometimes used for lining some of the simpler types of fireplaces which are not intensively used and which are not doused with water. This type of construction is not recommended. In localities where lava rock may be procured easily, the lava rock lining is equally as acceptable as fire-clay brick. Ordinary brick will shatter and disintegrate if subjected to extreme and sudden changes in temperature caused by water dousing.

Fire-clay brick (sometimes called fire brick) is made from fire clay by what is known as a dry pressing process. In this process, 4 or 5 percent of water by volume is added to the dry fire clay which, when thus moistened, seems hardly damp. The thoroughly mixed fire clay is then formed into bricks under a pressure estimated to approximate 4,000 to 5,000 pounds per square inch.

Fire clay, from which fire-clay brick is made is defined by the American Society for Testing Materials as a "sedimentary clay of low flux content, and consisting essentially of hydrosilicate of alumina." There are at least six or eight distinct kinds of fire clay, having different properties with respect to chemical composition.

The standard size of fire-clay brick is 9 by $4\frac{1}{2}$ by $2\frac{1}{2}$ inches. There are four classes of fire-clay brick, classified according to heat resistance. The class commonly known as third quality fire-clay brick, or correctly designated as moderate-heat-duty brick (according to the standard definition), is generally used for lining fireboxes and hearths in camp stoves and fireplaces. The softening point of this brick is approximately 2,905° F. and its maximum expansion is one-sixteenth inch per foot at a temperature of approximately 2,200°. Concrete will seldom withstand a temperature in excess of 1,000° F. and the normal temperature in the average camp stove or fireplace ranges from 800° to approximately 1,500°. The coefficient of expansion of fire-clay brick is about one-third or one-fourth of the coefficient of expansion of iron. In decimal figures, this coefficient is 0.000005 for each degree centigrade.

Fire-clay brick is usually laid on its natural bed, but sometimes it is laid on side. In laying fire-clay brick in camp stoves and fireplaces which are exposed to the weather, the fire-clay mortar should be a mixture of fire clay with approximately 20 to 25 percent of portland cement by bulk. This mortar is "buttered" lightly with a trowel on the surfaces of the brick and should make a joint approximately one-sixteenth inch in thickness. If the fire clay is spread too thickly, it will destroy the strength of the fire-clay brick lining. This joint should be just as thin as it is practicable to make it.

The reason for keeping fire-clay mortar very thin on the surface of the bricks is because the fire clay used in the joint between the bricks is not as resistant to heat as is the fire-clay brick itself. The joint would, therefore, have a tendency to shrink and cause damage if the joint were even as thick as one-fourth of an inch. This thin joint is sometimes procured by dipping the fire-clay brick in fire clay of a rich, creamy consistency and pushing the brick into place by rubbing the top brick back and forth on the lower brick.

Many instances are observed in which apparent defective construction has not produced satisfactory results in the construction of the fire-clay brick lining.

For the best results, fire clay used to create a bond between fire-clay brick should be subjected to a temperature exceeding 1,600° to 1,800° F. in order to cause the chemical reaction required to make the joint permanent. It is doubtful if the heat produced through the normal use of any firebox is sufficient to cause the permanent chemical change necessary to produce the desired result.

The best results are procured in the construction of fireboxes for outdoor camp stoves and fireplaces when, to the fire clay, there is added by volume approximately 20 to 25 percent of portland cement or similar cement. The addition of this cement produces a "cold set", which the subsequent heat further fixes, with the result that this fire clay and cement joint creates a solid and permanent bond.

It is desirable, in any event, whether or not cement is added to the fire clay, to subject the lining of the fireplace to an intense fire for at least 4 or 5 hours. If fire clay is used without the addition of cement, this fire should be sufficiently intense and continued sufficiently long so that the inside surface of the brick shows evidences of starting to glow. Unless this procedure is adopted the joint will be damaged by rain and by freezing.

There are on the market air-setting, high-temperature cements which will create an excellent bond under a cold set. It is doubtful if high-temperature cements will be as permanent as the bond produced by a mixture of fire clay and portland cement or its equivalent, as above suggested.

The average mortar will not usually withstand any considerable amount of heat because of the content of lime which fluxes under heat and because of the content of sand which does not have refractory qualities to the extent required in these joints.

In filling the space between the back of the fire-clay brick lining and the face of the stone masonry shell or covering, the fire clay, properly moistened, should be mixed with pulverized calsined fire clay in the proportions of one part fire clay to two or three parts of the calsined fire clay. It is not recommended that this space be filled with pure fire clay for the reason that the natural fire clay will shrink to a considerable extent when subjected to intense heat. The fire clay should be mixed as above indicated with calsined clay because the calsined clay has been subjected to a considerable heat and will therefore not be subject to any considerable amount of shrinking.

The space between the fire-clay brick lining and the stone masonry backing must be completely grouted and thoroughly sealed at the top to prevent any water from entering. In some camp stoves where intense heat is developed, an air space between the fire-clay brick lining and the face of the stone masonry is provided. This method of construction is open to some question. Sometimes this air space is filled with powdered asbestos in order to further protect the stone masonry against intense heat.

It is also advisable to construct the hearth, or floor of the firebox, with fire-clay brick unless, as in the fireplace shown on plate VII, figure 6, the surface of the hearth is level with the surrounding ground, in which case it may be equally as well constructed of mineral earth or natural porous soil.

In the fireplace with closed back (pls. III, IV, V, etc.), the only real draft control is in the orientation with respect to the direction of the prevailing wind. A raised back somewhat improves the draft, and a movable solid plate may sometimes be used in connection with the raised back to further control the draft.

The chimney notch shown in plate VIII increases the draft by restricting the gases to a definite limited passage. The maximum control of draft is obtained where a chimney is used. The draft is further controlled by dampers in the doors at the front of the firebox and also by dampers in the chimney. The chimney may vary in height, as shown in plates X and XII.

The door on the front of the firebox may be of cast iron or sheet iron, in conformity with the materials used for the cooking top. Besides being hinged so that it can be fully opened there may be, as shown in plate XXII–A, figs. 3, 4, and 5, a small opening in the door to provide draft.

A draft control necessary to maintain the desired fire may be provided in one of three ways as follows:

A. By an ashpit under the firebox, on the front of which is a door which may be opened or closed to produce greater or less draft.

B. By an opening in the door as shown in plate XXII–A, figures 3, 4, and 5.

C. By a damper constructed in the chimney (pl. XXII, fig. 3), or by a damper constructed in the rear of the firebox at the point where the flue enters the chimney.

It is apparently necessary in some localities of extreme moisture conditions, and especially in high altitudes where much fog is prevalent, to procure a maximum draft by providing an ashpit under the firebox. The ashpit is not generally recommended nor usually essential in the average camp stove. It ought not to be constructed unless the requirements for maximum draft, to burn wood not thoroughly dry, make such an ashpit indispensable.

Under normal conditions, sufficient draft control may be had through the adjustment of the doors in the firebox. Sometimes the draft in the chimney is controlled by a pivoted iron plate on the top of the chimney. The value of this device is open to question. The built-in type of damper with the revolving metal shield (pl. XXII, fig. 3) is the most effective; but its operation is not fool-proof. No damper should be installed which does not leave a limited portion of the flue (approximately 35 percent of its area) free when the damper is practically closed.

TOP GRATE OR TOP PLATE

The top of the stove or fireplace may consist of a grate (simple bars or a fabricated grate) or a solid plate. In some instances, in place of a definite grate a heavy electric welded wire mesh is being used. This type of grate is less expensive than the iron plate. The solid plate provides better draft and a better control over the draft. Its use reduces the fire hazard and is sometimes necessary in certain locations where the fire hazard is great. In some States laws have been enacted making it compulsory to use on camp stoves a solid plate for the top of the stove and a door on the front of the firebox which at all times prevents any possibility for sparks to escape and cause a forest fire. In picnic fireplaces, except those used for warming purposes, the grate is generally adopted but in a few instances a solid plate is used. On camp stoves, where the camper desires to keep the pots and pans from smudging, a solid plate is generally used. In many instances, and where the use justifies the expense, a combination grate and plate top is used (pls. X and III–A).

In some fireplaces, a successful method of cooking is that of using a reflector plate of sheet iron or other metal, which can be stood at an angle of approximately 60° immediately in front of the opening of the fireplace, and supported by an arm which keeps the plate at the proper position in relation to the fire. This contrivance is often used in place of a grate or plate over the top of the fire, and it may be home-made or purchased from some supply houses with the necessary attachments to hold food which would otherwise be laid upon the grate or plate. This method of cooking avoids unnecessary burning of food and is almost as efficient as the method of cooking food over the top of the fire.

Where the combination plate and grate is used, the plate may be used over a part of the grate as shown on plate III–A, figures 1 and 3. Such an arrangement makes possible an area for warming and grilling, and also an area for frying and other cooking.

In instances where the plate is used to cover the entire grate, both the grate and the plate may be hinged as shown in plate X, figure 4, or both the plate and the grate may be attached by a chain to the sides of the fireplace (pl. VII).

The plate is, without a doubt, the ideal top for a camp stove where the stove is used for three meals during each day. In picnic areas, where the fireplace is used for cooking purposes, perhaps once during the day and possibly not every day, a grate or mesh is acceptable, although the extra work of cleaning blackened pots and pans is necessary. The fabricated grate or mesh (pl. VI) is much preferable to built-in bars shown in plate IV.

It is very important that the space between the bars in any grate be not too large, thus allowing small sections of meat to fall between the bars. The average acceptable space between bars is 1¾ inches. The use of separate bars, although not the most acceptable solution, is sometimes necessary where, either because of lack of funds or for other reasons, a suitable fabricated grate or mesh cannot be procured.

The bars to be of proper strength should be approximately ½ to ¾ inch square, or they may be circular, with a diameter of ¾ to 1 inch.

The plate ought to be of sheet iron or cast iron. Ten-gage black iron or boilerplate offers a quick heating surface. Cast-iron plate, if too thick, usually heats too slowly. A normal thickness is three-eighths inch.

Considerable difficulty may be experienced because of the tendency of any top plate of sheet iron to warp and sag. This undesirable result is caused by the following conditions:

A. Using a plate of iron which is too thin.
B. Not using the necessary angle irons or other methods of reenforcing the top plate.

C. Making no provision for expansion at the points where the plate is attached to the masonry construction.

Removable cast-iron plates are not as practical as sheet-iron plates for the reason that the rough handling which is received by some of these movable tops will cause breakage. In all removable plates there should be one or more holes at some convenient location to facilitate handling. The cast-iron tops may sometimes be fitted with pot holes of various sizes, each of which is covered with a lid or sheet-iron plate, all of which must be securely anchored to prevent removal or loss. Such small movable parts are not entirely practical in the average campground and their use should be discouraged.

Steel plates should not be used because steel rusts easily when exposed to the weather, unless protected with paint and carefully maintained.

Flanges at the edges of the plates as shown in plate VIII, figure 1 and in plate XXII, figure 4 and extending entirely across the firebox will do much to prevent sagging. The problem of warping is one which comes from exposure to heat and is not due to any great extent to the inability of the plate to support itself. Proper reenforcing on the underside of the plate and correct attachment of the plate to the masonry sides of the stove or fireplace will overcome it.

A desirable method for attaching any plate to the solid masonry is to provide proper reenforcing members on the underside of the plate, the end of which will fit into a metal socket similar to that shown in plate XXI, figure 5, thus allowing for the necessary expansion and preventing any damage to the stone masonry at this point. Where bars are used, the ends of the bars should fit into pipe sleeves of somewhat large diameter and with ample clearance allowed in order to provide for the expansion (pl. IV, fig. 4). Provision may be made as shown in plate XXI, figure 5B, for the removal and replacement of bars which are broken or bent through careless use of the fireplace. Where bars are used in place of a fabricated grate, it is sometimes desirable to carry the bars in sockets entirely through the stone masonry wall, as shown in plate XXI, figure 5C. In cases where this method of construction is adopted, some provision should be made for locking the bars so that they cannot be easily removed. This is accomplished as shown in plate XXI, figure 5, section A–A. Attaching bars and grates solidly to masonry will break the stone. If a fixed grate is used, the grate may be so constructed that the corners will have bars which fit into metal sleeves as above described. As a matter of fact, the top plate and any bars should never be attached in a fixed manner to the top of the stone masonry. Suitable provision should be made to take care of expansion. Where the grate is removable it can rest on a base formed by the top layer of fire-clay brick as shown in plate VII.

The question of whether to use a removable or a fixed top has not been satisfactorily solved as a result of experience to date. The removable top increases the convenience of building fires and removing ashes. The fixed top on the other hand, is an additional safeguard against vandalism and otherwise careless use of these facilities.

Where a solid plate is used, especially in fireplaces, it is desirable that this plate be removable or hinged so that the fireplace may be used as an open warming fire during the evenings and on cool days at times when the fireplace is not in use for actual cooking purposes.

If the top is removable, it should be securely attached with a chain, anchored to the masonry, or to a post driven in the ground to a sufficient depth to prevent any removal of this feature.

Where a hinge is used for attaching the plate or grate to the top of the stove or fireplace, the type of construction as shown in plates VI and X is most acceptable. If the top grate or plate is to be hinged, this detail of construction should be solid, and of such a type that damage cannot be easily caused by careless handling. See detail of hinge in plate XXI, figures 2, 3, and 4.

As shown in plate IV, it is sometimes necessary to sink the grate or plate slightly below the level of the side "shoulders" in order to provide for the proper anchoring of the hinges or the bars. The elevation of the side walls may also give some small protection, especially to the fire when the grate is used.

In many camp stoves and in fireplaces with a solid top, an abnormal amount of heat is lost because it passes up the chimney. This condition can be corrected to a large extent by the construction of a proper damper in the chimney and by the construction of a shallow firebox with a larger heating surface, as shown in plate XIII. In some areas where the proper provision is not made to prevent an abnormal amount of heat from passing up the chimney, many efficient campers set some of the pots and other cooking utensils on the top of the chimney in order to take advantage of the heat at that point.

In most camp stoves and fireplaces the limited space on the top of the cooking surface is not sufficient to set all of the pots and pans in which food is being cooked or being kept warm. Additional space may be provided as shown in plates VI, VII, and VIII, with very little additional cost.

STONEWORK

There are many kinds of stone available in different parts of the country from which to construct camp stoves and fireplaces. This stone ranges from the "nigger heads" and boulders of the New England region to the lava rock of the Northwest and the Tufa rock of the extreme South.

The detailed design and construction of any stove or fireplace, of which various types are shown in the following plates, will vary with the kind of local stone which can be procured. The same design, built of volcanic rock, will take on a different texture and appearance from the one constructed of stratified sandstone or of boulders. The carrying out of each design in the materials available and in the most appropriate form must, to considerable extent, be left to the judgment of the local superintendent.

All stonework should be constructed as closely as practicable in accordance with the detailed drawings. A special effort should be made to procure an informal texture with stones laid on their natural bed in order to carry the horizontal effect (pls. XXIV and XXV). There may be rare instances in which the surrounding natural conditions require that the stone be laid to produce a vertical texture.

17

All stone before being laid should be free from any dirt or foreign matter and, unless the supply of stone is extremely limited, it is much better to select individual stones of the size and shape which will produce the required texture of stonework than to endeavor to use the large and the small stones as they are found.

Stones which are cut or broken are usually divided into two classes: (a) Stratified; (b) Unstratified.

The examples of stratified stone are sandstones, limestones, and shales. Igneous rock, granite, and lava are in the unstratified group.

Stratified stone (pl. XXV, fig. 5) is easier to lay than the unstratified stone (pl. XXIV, fig. 5), which requires a more careful selection to produce desired effect in actual construction.

Stone texture is an elusive element in design because so much depends on the skill of the workmen. A camp stove or fireplace must be practical in use, and it must be of appropriate design in mass and texture. The texture of the stone masonry is so frequently not well designed (pl. XXIV, and pl. XXV, figs. 2, 4, and 6), that its importance in the completed structure should not be minimized. Many of these features look like stone piles with no stability or like monoliths of mortar and stone with no surface texture.

Joints in stonework should be neat and approximately ½ to ¾ inch wide. The color of the mortar used in the joints should blend with the natural color of the stone. In well-constructed stone masonry, the mortar is not conspicuous. In any event, the mortar should not be colored unless it is necessary to avoid unusually light color which contrasts unnecessarily with the color of the stonework. These joints should be raked fairly deep in order to eliminate so far as possible the effect of too much mortar, and to produce the effect of a natural dry stone wall.

CHIMNEYS

The chimney does not add to the attractiveness of any fireplace or camp stove. In fact, it is a rather unattractive feature which increases the massiveness, and for this reason it should be avoided whenever practical. A low chimney is sometimes not entirely effective, and, on the other hand, if sufficiently high to function satisfactorily the chimney may dominate the unit.

The chimney, when used, may range from the simple funnel (pl. XXVI, figs. 9, 10, and 11) on the "ice box" and "oil drum" types of camp stoves to a definite masonry construction, as shown in plates XI and XII. It is confined usually to the camp stove. A low chimney may sometimes be constructed on a fireplace of the types shown in plates X and XI. This feature is most essential where the fire hazard is very great.

The height of the chimney should be kept to a minimum and may vary from 2 feet above ground, as shown in plate X, to 6 or 7 feet, as shown in plate XIII.

When the fire hazard is much above normal, the chimney should be provided with a damper control, and sometimes with a spark arrester (pl. XXII, fig. 3, and pl. XIII, fig. 3).

If the spark arrester is not used, there is great danger that the live sparks may be carried into highly inflammable timber. The spark arrester is a small mesh of woven wire screen in a frame, held in place at the top of the flue by means of prongs or clamps. It should be installed in such a way that its condition may be easily inspected and its replacement made simple.

The throat of the fireplace is that portion leading from the firebox to the chimney flue. In the regular indoor fireplace (pl. XXIII) the opening of the throat is about equal to the area of the flue and is the full width of the fireplace. In the camp stove fireplace (pl. XII), here discussed, the full width may not always be obtainable, but the proper area should be maintained, and so far as possible the width of the throat should be greater than its height (pl. XIII, fig. 3).

The chimney flue should in every instance be lined with a fire-clay brick or with some other regular lining. The height of the chimney, the size of the firebox, and the ashpit, as well as exposure, and type of vegetation surrounding the camp unit are important factors in the control of the draft. In general the area of the horizontal section of a round or a square flue from a single firebox should be not less than one-tenth of the transverse vertical section of the combined firebox and ashpit. An arbitrary minimum area for the flue might be 4 inches square. A rectangular flue should somewhat exceed the minimum area above stated. In camp stoves with open fronts on the firebox, the flue area should be further increased as indicated by drawings. A flue which is too large in relation to the firebox, tends to create a sluggish fire. In determining the size of flue for camp stoves other than for specific ones illustrated in this bulletin, use these illustrations as a guide.

In the multiple-unit type of camp stove, with a single square flue, properly lined, division by galvanized metal partitions into the proper number of smaller flues of proper sizes and each serving its own firebox, is essential (pl. XIII, fig. 4). This arrangement will prevent cold air from being drawn in from any unused firebox, thereby lessening the draft from the burning fire. The metal partitions will ultimately rust out and must be replaced. The installation of any damper in the chimney should be in accordance with drawings shown in plate XXII, figure 3.

MATERIALS FOR CONSTRUCTION

THE appearance and the permanency of camp stoves and fireplaces are increased greatly if the materials for construction are selected with proper care. The more important materials include the following:

  A. Iron (for top grates, plates, doors, hinges, etc.).
  B. Brick (for fireboxes and flues).
  C. Concrete (for foundations).
  D. Stone (for masonry construction and dry stone construction).
  E. Sand (for mixtures of concrete and for hearths).

IRON AND BRICK

Iron and brick have been discussed in foregoing parts of this bulletin.

BRICK

See discussion under Fireboxes.

CONCRETE

Concrete should seldom be considered except for foundations. Mixtures for concrete are discussed under Foundations.

STONE

The natural climatic conditions may be injurious to some kinds of stone, especially shales. In locations where water will be used generally to extinguish the fire, very careful consideration should be given to the kinds of stone to be selected for the proposed construction. In the order of their resistance to heat the acceptable kinds of stone are the following:

  A. Dense black lava rock.
  B. Fine grained sandstone.
  C. Coarse grained sandstone.
  D. Granite.
  E. Limestone.
  F. Laminated shale and river stone.

Limestones and shales are most undesirable because of the damaging effects of intense heat. These stones have a large calcium carbonate content. Granite will to some extent "flake", and may crack. If the firebox is lined with fire-clay brick, providing a means of protecting these stones from intense heat or sudden changes of extreme temperatures, any of the stones in this list will be acceptable.

Sandstones when procured with fine grain will withstand the heat in an excellent manner. They are composed of fine sand which is held together by some substances of a cementing character, usually silica, alumina, or oxide of lime. Those with the silica content are much more desirable.

Granite is formed by volcanic action and is among the igneous rocks composed of quartz, felspar and mica. Because of the quartz content this rock has good resistance to heat. On the other hand, this type of stone is much more difficult to cut than sandstone.

Slate is not a heat resistant stone and is subject to damage under high temperature.

A portland cement mortar, or a mortar of similar qualities is desirable. The mix should consist of one part cement, one part fire clay, and five parts sand. A small amount of hydrated lime may be added to prevent the mortar from setting too quickly. This, however, should be used very sparingly and is not essential. Mix thoroughly before adding water.

SAND

There are two kinds of sand which may be procured for mortar, as follows:

  A. Pit sand or bank sand.
  B. River or lake sand.

The difference between these two types of sand is as follows:

The river sand is generally free from any clay content. The grains are less angular and in general it is less desirable for use in mortar.

Pit or bank sand usually has a small clay or loam content which must be washed from it in order to get the particles of sand clean. The particles of sand are angular and somewhat rough and therefore make it much more desirable for mortar making.

Sand which is used for the hearth and also for the area around the fireplace should have a small proportion (approximately 10 to 15 percent) of clay content, in order that there may be some cementing quality in this mixture—otherwise the sand will not pack and become firm under foot, especially around the fireplace.

DETAILED DISCUSSION
OF SPECIFIC TYPES

ADAPTATION TO LOCATION AND USE

•

DESIGN AND CONSTRUCTION

•

VARIATIONS IN DESIGN

ON THE following plates are shown different types of camp stoves and fireplaces, ranging from the very elementary and primitive type (pl. I, fig. 1), to the very "sophisticated" and artificial type (pl. I, fig. 2). In connection with each specific type of camp stove and fireplace, there is presented a discussion of the problems of adaptation to location and use, and of the problems of design and construction.

In the minds of some readers, these drawings may indicate in some instances solutions which seem rather ideal, and not capable of practical application because of the fact that the most desirable kinds and shapes of stones necessary to produce the effect shown in the drawings are not available. These drawings are intended to show only in a general way the kind of design which may be followed in actual construction. Minor modifications are often necessary on account of varying materials and conditions on different areas in different parts of the country.

The success or failure in procuring the kind of results illustrated in the drawings depends upon the ability of the man who is superintending the construction work in the field, and of the stone mason who is doing the work of actual construction.

TYPES OF FIREPLACES

THE simple types shown in figures 1, 3, 4, 5, and 6B, are appropriate for forest picnic areas. They are not adapted for camp grounds except where the camper desires to accept the natural inconvenience accompanying "life in the wild." Their simplicity, crudeness of construction, and inconspicuous mass are strongly in their favor.

FIGURE 1

Crude Fireplace of Boulders or Rocks Loosely Piled in the Shape of a Horseshoe.—This type is not conspicuous; it is inconvenient in use and creates an abnormal fire hazard. It has a place on large open picnic areas because it is not conspicuous. If this is the only type of fireplace provided on the camp grounds, the majority of the campers and picnickers will use some kind of a portable gas stove (pl. I, fig. 2) for cooking purposes. The construction of this type of fireplace will vary, depending on the available stone (whether of the boulder type or of the stratified type). In portions of the country where a stratified stone is available, a few flat stones might be used on which to set pots and pans for warming purposes.

This fireplace is adapted for use as a campfire for light, and especially for warmth in the cool evening hours. In the eastern part of the country, where such a large percentage (in some instances more than 80 percent) of the campers use portable stoves, it is a most practical feature to supplement the gasoline stove.

FIGURE 2

Portable Gasoline Stove.—This stove is frequently used by campers and picnickers especially where there is a scarcity of fuel and lack of properly designed camp stoves and fireplaces adapted for convenient use. It has limited cooking surface, provides quick heat for cooking, and it is also of practical value in rainy weather.

FIGURE 3

Fireplace Cut in Rock Ledge.—This type of fireplace is very attractive, but often destructive of the natural beauty of the rock out-crop. Such a fireplace is often expensive to construct. It cannot be conveniently used from the sides, and therefore must be of minimum length (15 to 18 inches). A grate of desired length similar to the grate shown in figure 4 may be used. The grate on such a fireplace must be movable, and attached to the ledge with a chain. In ledge rock which will not withstand extremely high temperatures, it is desirable to construct a fire-clay brick lining in order to protect the stone in the natural ledge.

FIGURE 4

Artificial Ledge Effect.—The proposed grate may be either a standard grate such as shown in figure 6B, or a movable grate chained to the rock. In localities where a suitable type of ledge rock is available, the construction of this type of fireplace may not involve an abnormal expense, and may be a most interesting feature.

FIGURE 5

Open End Single Stone Type.—This is the simplest form of open fireplace, and is to be strongly discouraged where fire hazard is present. If the stones are carefully selected, this fireplace is desirable for use on open picnic areas.

FIGURE 6

Standard Grates.—This figure shows three kinds of standard grates often used for picnic purposes. Each is simple in design, and not unduly conspicuous.

Type "C" is a simple grate with sheet iron sides. Type "B" is the same kind of a grate with large rocks at each side. The grate in each of these fireplaces is supported by four legs, each of which may be solidly anchored as shown on plate III, figures 4 and 5. Type "B" is the

CRUDE FIREPLACE
FIG 1

PORTABLE GASOLINE STOVE
FIG 2

TYPES OF FIREPLACES

FIREPLACE CUT IN ROCK LEDGE
FIG 3

ARTIFICIAL LEDGE EFFECT
FIG 4

OPEN END SINGLE STONE TYPE
FIG 5

STANDARD GRATES
FIG 6

PLATE I

more appropriate type. The grate marked "A" is not desirable except on intensively used picnic areas where the occupancy varies from that of maximum use to that of little use on successive days or week-ends. There is to date little reason for using such a portable unit in the forest recreation areas. In practical use the fire is started, and the grate is placed over it.

Simple fireplaces of the types similar to figures 5 and 6B should be adopted generally for use in designated locations on the "Primitive areas", where some crude fireplace facilities must be provided; but limited to only such as are absolutely necessary for fire protection. There are certain strategic places even in these areas where hikers and canoeists must camp, and without some such facilities for simple cooking these practically unprotected areas would be in danger of fire.

OPEN END MASONRY FIREPLACE

ADAPTATION TO LOCATION AND USE

The open ends may provide a better draft in locations where the prevailing winds are in opposite directions in the morning and in the evening, and may further vary during the day. This type is ordinarily used with a grate. A solid plate, attached to the stonework by a chain could, when not used as a cooking top, be set up against one end of the fireplace to control the draft. It is excellently adapted for use on large open picnic areas because it is low and not conspicuous. The disadvantage of this type is that a strong current of air will scatter the sparks and create a definite fire hazard.

DESIGN AND CONSTRUCTION

The stonework on the sides should be informal and rustic so far as the available material will allow, and should conceal the fire-clay brick lining and soften the general appearance.

A "floating pad foundation", reinforced as shown in the drawings, consisting of a concrete slab, the top of which is placed slightly below ground level, is required. This type of foundation will heave and settle under frost action without damaging the stone masonry superstructure. It is not essential in this type of fireplace to carry the foundation walls below the frost line.

The hearth of the firebox is slightly (1 to 2 inches) above the ground level and may be constructed of porous soil, mineral earth, or fire-clay brick. The hearth should be raised in the middle and pitched towards either end in order to provide proper drainage.

The open-ended firebox (approximating 10 inches in height) will accommodate longer lengths of wood than the three sided type (pl. III). This firebox should be lined with fire-clay brick and in the absence of any connecting end

to bond the sides together, provision should be made to bond the fire-clay brick into the stone masonry walls by the use of headers as shown in figure 3 of this plate. The four courses of fire-clay brick laid on their natural bed will slightly exceed 10 inches in height, while two courses laid edgewise will slightly exceed 9 inches in height.

A type of stone should be selected which will resist heat. The width of the stone sides should be kept to minimum dimensions, approximating from 6 to 10 inches. Any standard type of grate may be used. The grate shown is hinged on ⅜-inch "I" bolts set into the joints, as shown on plate XXII, figure 1.

Some park authorities have experimented with the open-end fireplace constructed with concrete sides, and with the bars embedded solidly in the concrete walls. In every instance, the expansion of the iron has caused the concrete to break.

VARIATIONS IN DESIGN

A movable grate, securely attached to the stonework (pl. VII) may be substituted for the hinged grate shown in this drawing.

The stonework in the side walls may be kept at the elevation of the top of the fire-clay brick, if a movable plate or grate is used, in order to regulate heating of dishes and utensils by placing them partly on the grate or plate and partly on the side walls. This method of construction would weaken the bond between the fire-clay brick and the stonework.

The brick hearth may be omitted and a fill of sand or of mineral earth may be used in its place. If such construction is adopted, then the foundation under each side wall should be carried below the frost line (in lieu of a reinforced concrete pad).

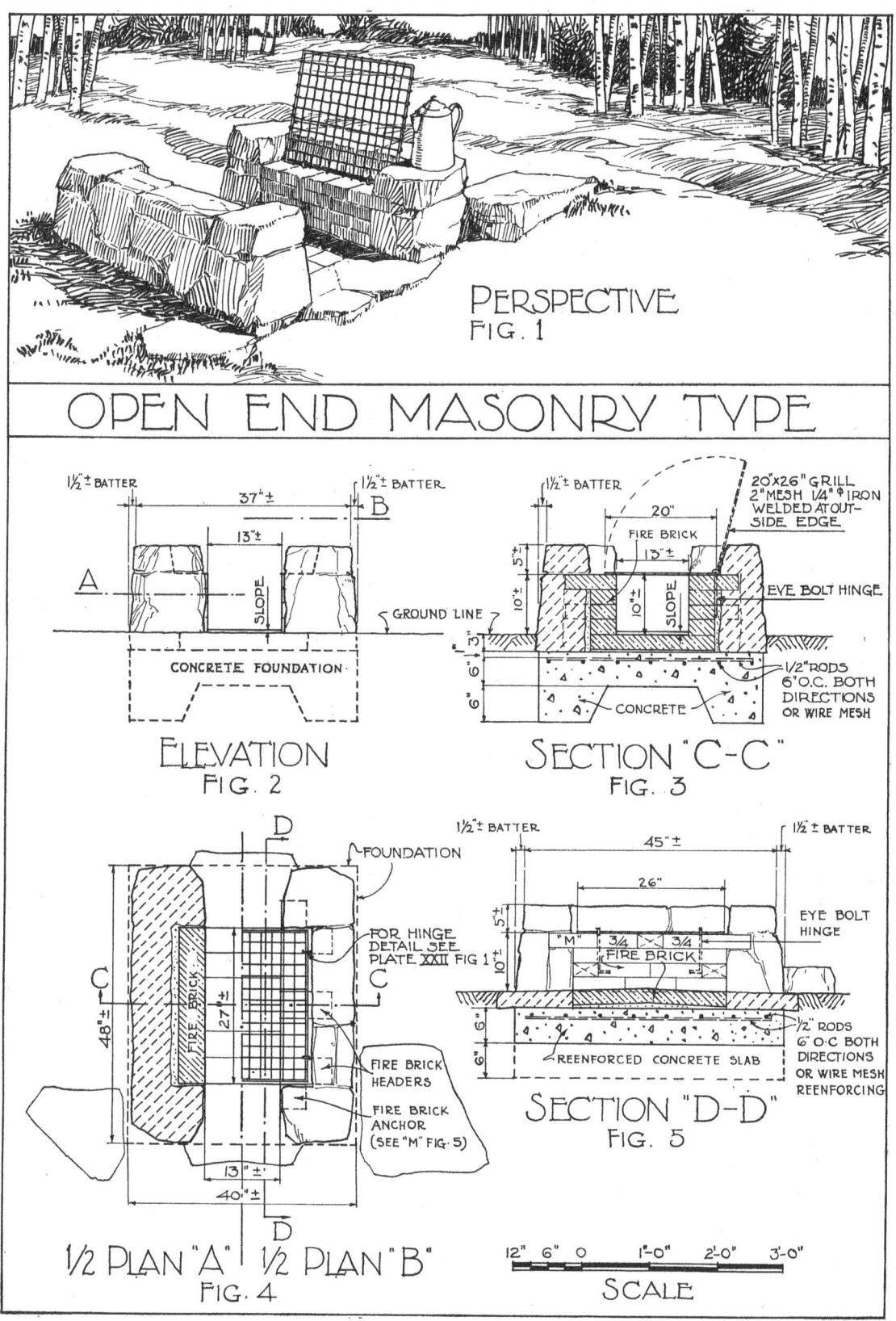

PERSPECTIVE
FIG. 1

OPEN END MASONRY TYPE

ELEVATION
FIG. 2

SECTION "C-C"
FIG. 3

½ PLAN "A" ½ PLAN "B"
FIG. 4

SECTION "D-D"
FIG. 5

SCALE

PLATE II

ROCK SLAB FIREPLACE

ADAPTATION TO LOCATION AND USE

This fireplace of simple design and construction is not massive. It is low and inconspicuous and well adapted for picnic use, especially in areas where the fire hazard is small. The open end should be toward the prevailing wind. This type without removable plate is not well adapted for use on camp grounds. (See pl. III–A.)

Since the construction of this fireplace is dependent upon the availability of the desired kind of large stones, laid without mortar, its adaptation to certain sites is limited.

Some question has been raised concerning the problem of maintenance in this fireplace, where the intense heat comes in direct contact with the stone, and especially where it is necessary to douse the fire. If the proper kind of heat-resisting stone is available (as described under "Stone"), the maintenance expense should be no greater than in any other fireplace. Sometimes a sheet iron plate is used on either side of the standard grate in order to protect the stone against the heat (pl. III–A, fig. 2).

DESIGN AND CONSTRUCTION

The grate is entirely separate from the rock. These rocks should be somewhat irregular, with the exception that the ends should be roughly dressed, as should the top (to provide a shelf on which to set pots and pans). The rock used in this fireplace must be of the heat-resisting kind. The stones on either side are sunk about one-half of their height into the ground and the tops of the stones are level with the top of the grate. The ends of the stone should be set as close together as possible in order to prevent a cross draft in the firebox. They can easily be replaced if damaged by heat and water.

The grate is anchored by being attached to a concrete block as shown on figure 4, or by being attached to a "log dead-man" (fig. 6). The hearth is usually made of sand or mineral earth and is level with surrounding ground.

The length and width of the firebox is dependent upon the size of the standard grate which is adopted. The height of the firebox should be normal, that is 9 to 12 inches.

VARIATIONS IN DESIGN

Variations in design are shown in figure 2 on plate III, and also in plate III–A. Sometimes the stone at the end may project slightly above the top of the grate to form a raised back which has a tendency to improve the draft.

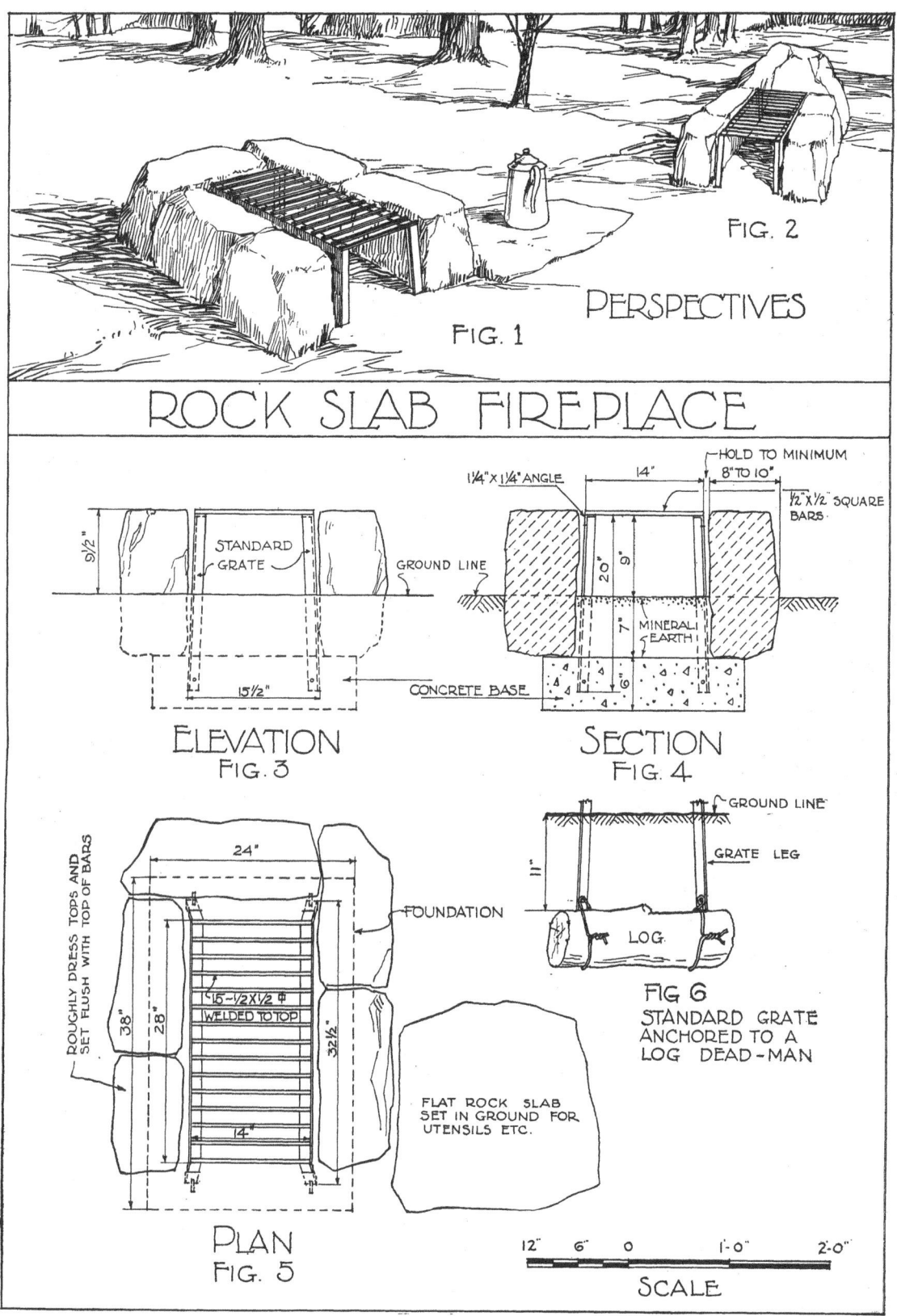

PERSPECTIVES

FIG. 2

FIG. 1

ROCK SLAB FIREPLACE

9½"

STANDARD GRATE

GROUND LINE

15½"

ELEVATION
FIG. 3

CONCRETE BASE

1¼" x 1¼" ANGLE

14"

HOLD TO MINIMUM 8" TO 10"

½" x ½" SQUARE BARS

20"

9"

7"

6"

MINERAL EARTH

SECTION
FIG. 4

ROUGHLY DRESS TOPS AND SET FLUSH WITH TOP OF BARS

24"

38"

28"

32½"

15 - ½ X ½ ∅ WELDED TO TOP

14"

FOUNDATION

FLAT ROCK SLAB SET IN GROUND FOR UTENSILS ETC.

PLAN
FIG. 5

GROUND LINE

GRATE LEG

11"

LOG.

FIG 6
STANDARD GRATE ANCHORED TO A LOG DEAD-MAN

12"   6"   0   1-0"   2-0"

SCALE

PLATE III

STANDARD GRATE
FIREPLACE VARIATIONS

ADAPTATION TO LOCATION AND USE

This type of fireplace may be developed in a number of ways as shown upon the accompanying plate. Its simplicity of design, permanence of grate, cheapness and ease of construction are important factors which increase its popularity. It is constructed in one form or another for use on picnic areas and on campgrounds, from California to Maine and from northern Washington to Florida. It is a comparatively inconspicuous unit, and for use in its simpler forms (as shown in pl. III, fig. 1; and pl. III–A, figs. 1, 2, and 3) in primitive areas and in high mountain country near timber line, it has no equal. As explained under plate III this unit is not recommended for use in areas of high fire hazard.

The type shown in figure 6 is also not recommended for use in areas where there is any tendency toward vandalism or any rough usage which might knock down the dry stone-enclosing wall. The types shown in figures 7 and 8 are excellently adapted for areas which are used at frequent intervals by rather large groups who frequently have "fish fries." These multiple units provide necessary increase in cooking surface and have proven to be very popular in actual use on a number of recreation areas. In multiple units such as shown in figure 8 the width of the top of the enclosing wall on either side of the large fireplace, may be narrow (approximating 6 inches) because of the reduced requirements for any "warming shelf", and because stones of the width normally used on either side of the single unit fireplace might cause inconvenience in the actual use of the fireplace.

Wherever the single units are used for campground cooking, it is generally desirable that a removable plate be used to cover a portion of the top of the grate as shown in figures 1 and 5.

DESIGN AND CONSTRUCTION

In addition to the comments with reference to the design and construction of this type of fireplace included under plates II and III, this further information may be of value.

This fireplace is sometimes designed as shown in figures 4 and 6 with the long side open to the front. When the fireplace is thus designed it is desirable that the top of the surrounding wall be slightly above the top of the grate and yet not exceeding 18 inches in the height inasmuch as a wall of greater height would not be convenient for use as a seat on which to sit while cooking food on the grate.

The efficiency of this fireplace is greatly increased by the use of the removable top plate.

Whenever a fire-clay brick lining is used in the firebox it is very desirable that the stone masonry construction protect and cover the ends of the fireplace lining as shown on the right-hand side of the fireplace in figure 5. The method of anchoring the standard grate is shown in plate III.

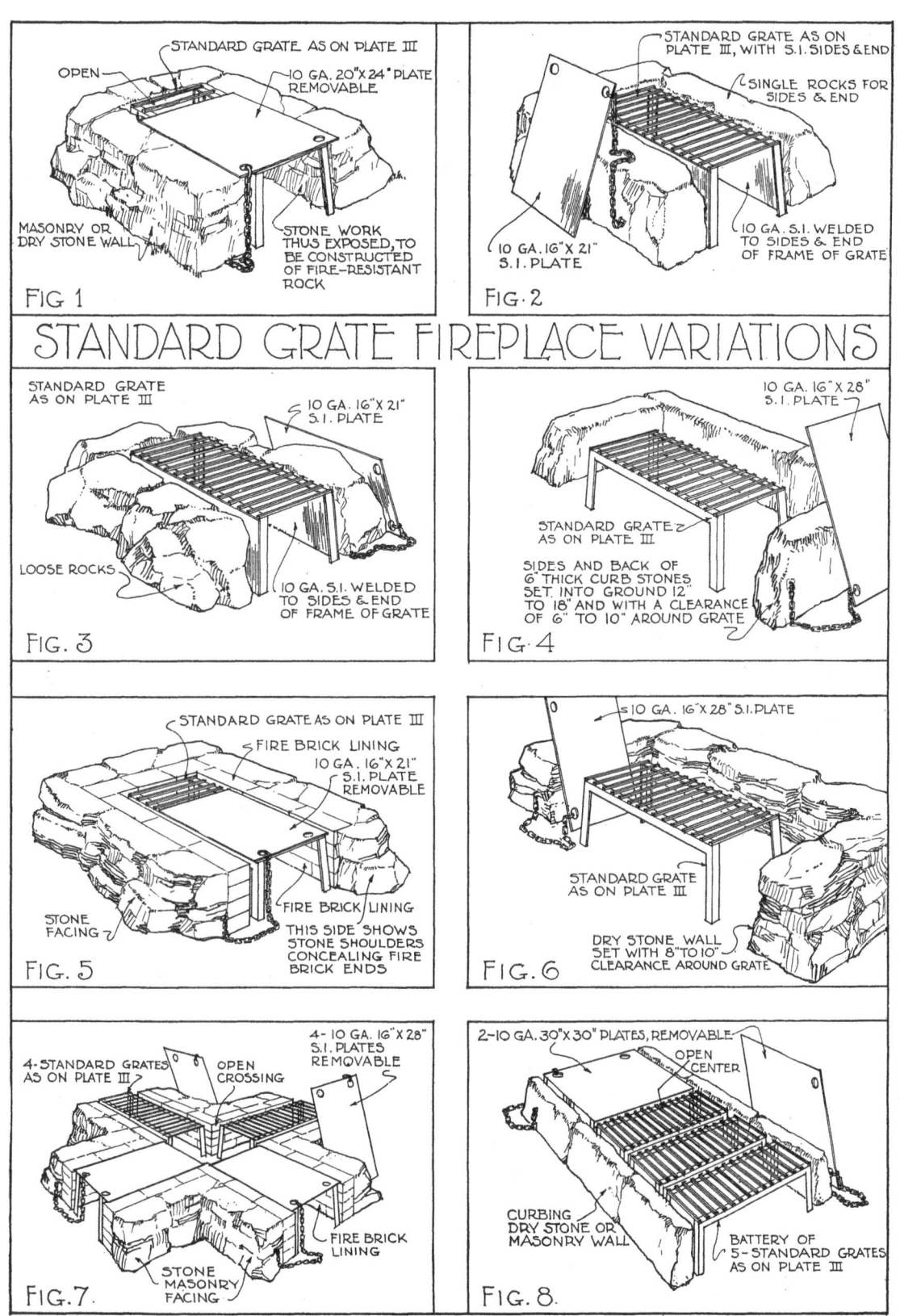

FIG 1
OPEN
STANDARD GRATE AS ON PLATE III
10 GA. 20"X 24" PLATE REMOVABLE
MASONRY OR DRY STONE WALL
STONE WORK THUS EXPOSED, TO BE CONSTRUCTED OF FIRE-RESISTANT ROCK

FIG. 2
STANDARD GRATE AS ON PLATE III, WITH S.I. SIDES & END
SINGLE ROCKS FOR SIDES & END
10 GA. 16"X 21" S.I. PLATE
10 GA. S.I. WELDED TO SIDES & END OF FRAME OF GRATE

STANDARD GRATE FIREPLACE VARIATIONS

FIG. 3
STANDARD GRATE AS ON PLATE III
10 GA. 16"X 21" S.I. PLATE
LOOSE ROCKS
10 GA. S.I. WELDED TO SIDES & END OF FRAME OF GRATE

FIG. 4
10 GA. 16"X 28" S.I. PLATE
STANDARD GRATE AS ON PLATE III
SIDES AND BACK OF 6" THICK CURB STONES SET INTO GROUND 12" TO 18" AND WITH A CLEARANCE OF 6" TO 10" AROUND GRATE

FIG. 5
STANDARD GRATE AS ON PLATE III
FIRE BRICK LINING
10 GA. 16"X 21" S.I. PLATE REMOVABLE
STONE FACING
FIRE BRICK LINING
THIS SIDE SHOWS STONE SHOULDERS CONCEALING FIRE BRICK ENDS

FIG. 6
10 GA. 16"X 28" S.I. PLATE
STANDARD GRATE AS ON PLATE III
DRY STONE WALL SET WITH 8"TO 10" CLEARANCE AROUND GRATE

FIG. 7.
4-STANDARD GRATES AS ON PLATE III
OPEN CROSSING
4- 10 GA. 16"X 28" S.I. PLATES REMOVABLE
FIRE BRICK LINING
STONE MASONRY FACING

FIG. 8.
2-10 GA. 30"X 30" PLATES, REMOVABLE
OPEN CENTER
CURBING DRY STONE OR MASONRY WALL
BATTERY OF 5-STANDARD GRATES AS ON PLATE III

PLATE III-A

INFORMAL FIREPLACE

ADAPTATION TO LOCATION AND USE

This informal fireplace is well adapted to the natural forest surroundings, especially if the stone used in its construction is carefully selected. In considering this fireplace for any specific area, the designer should determine in advance that stones of the character and size indicated in the drawings are available at a reasonable cost.

This type ought not to be used where the fire hazard is great. It is primarily adapted for picnic areas, rather than for campgrounds, although with a removable solid plate the variation shown in figure 2 could to excellent advantage be used on campgrounds.

DESIGN AND CONSTRUCTION

It has the appearance of dry stone masonry, although it is of solid masonry construction. The joints should be very narrow and raked deeply. The stonework in every way should present a natural appearance. It is important that the side walls be kept as low as practicable in order that the cooking surface be easily and conveniently accessible.

Figure 1 shows flat projecting rocks at the end and sides on which to set cooking utensils.

The foundation should consist of a "floating concrete pad", properly reenforced as shown. In some instances, especially where the hearth is of sand or mineral soil, the foundation under each side should be carried below frost (fig. 6).

The width and length of the firebox may be varied, depending upon the available supply of fuel. The grate consists of ¾-inch iron bars or pipe set in 1-inch sleeves at either end in order to avoid damage from expansion (pl. XXI, fig. 5).

VARIATIONS IN DESIGN

Figures 2 and 6 show the variations in design. A movable plate or grate may be substituted for the built-in bars, and this plate or grate should be attached securely with a chain. (See pl. XXI, figs. 1, 6, and 7.) If the stone masonry side walls are carried only to the height of the fire-clay brick lining it is necessary to take special precautions in constructing the top of joint between the fire-clay brick and stonework.

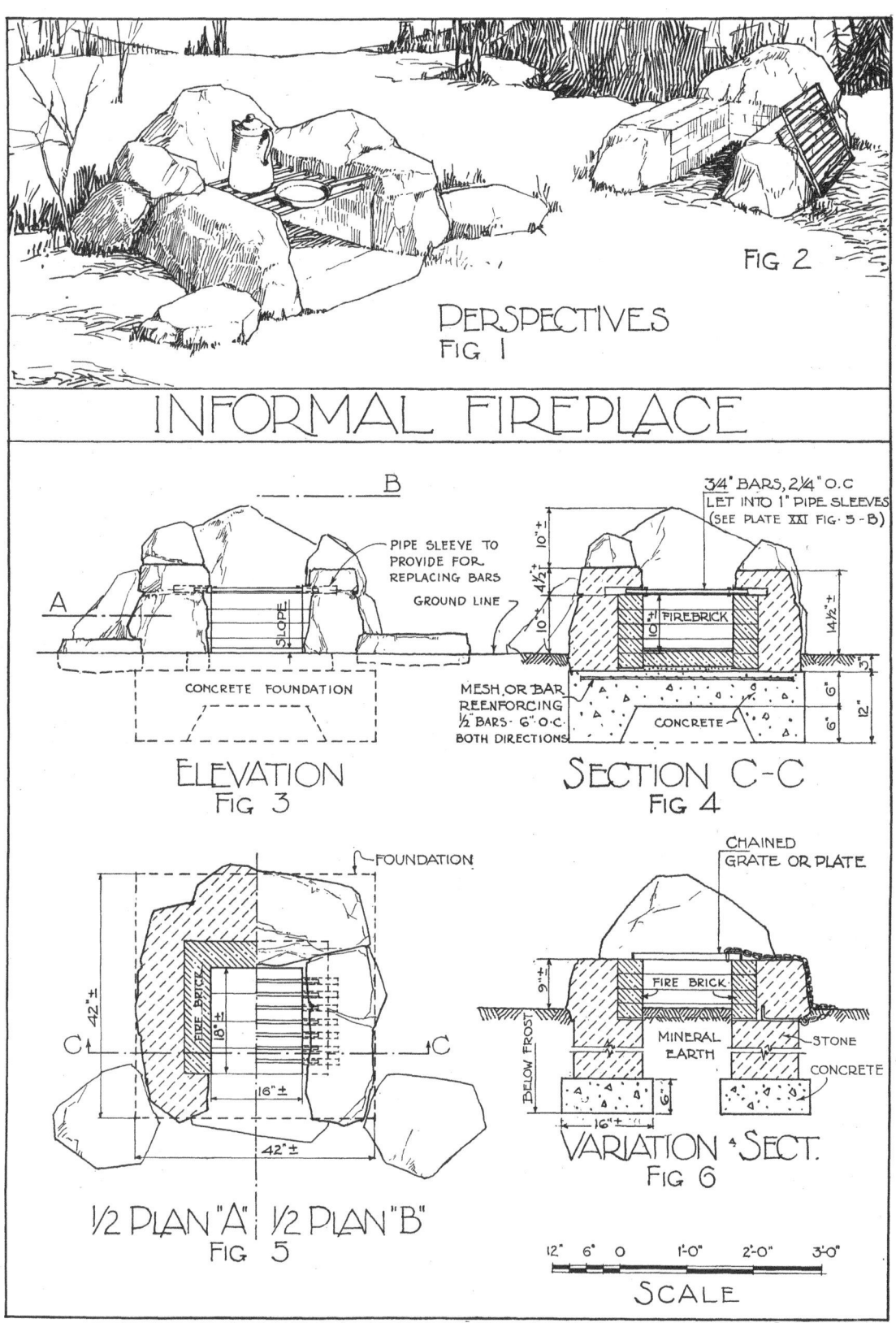

FIG 2

PERSPECTIVES
FIG 1

INFORMAL FIREPLACE

B

PIPE SLEEVE TO
PROVIDE FOR
REPLACING BARS

GROUND LINE

A

SLOPE

CONCRETE FOUNDATION

ELEVATION
FIG 3

3/4" BARS, 2 1/4" O.C
LET INTO 1" PIPE SLEEVES
(SEE PLATE XXI FIG. 5-B)

FIREBRICK

MESH OR BAR
REENFORCING
1/2 BARS. 6" O.C.
BOTH DIRECTIONS

CONCRETE

SECTION C-C
FIG 4

FOUNDATION

FIRE BRICK

42" ±

18"

C   C

16" ±

42" ±

1/2 PLAN "A" 1/2 PLAN "B"
FIG 5

CHAINED
GRATE OR PLATE

FIRE BRICK

BELOW FROST   9" ±

MINERAL
EARTH

STONE

CONCRETE

16" ±

VARIATION SECT.
FIG 6

12" 6" 0   1'-0"   2'-0"   3'-0"

SCALE

PLATE IV

33

WESTERN PICNIC FIREPLACE

THE fundamental design for this informal fireplace has been developed by the National Park Service and modified in minor detail for use in this volume. This fireplace is not a conspicuous unit, and is most appropriate to the natural forest surroundings where the fire hazard is not abnormally high.

The sides are splayed, as shown in the drawing, and the top of the firebox is covered with a solid plate. For picnic use only, the top might be covered with a removable grate, instead of a fixed plate. It is the author's observation that most recreationists prefer a solid plate, even for picnic use.

The small opening between the back of the plate and the fire-clay brick lining provides an opening which serves as a flue, especially with the back of the fireplace tilted slightly forward. (See fig. 3.) The firebox is lined with fire-clay brick on the sides and bottom. That portion of the bottom of the firebox extending in front of the top plate and on which little or no fire will exist, may be paved with stone.

DESIGN AND CONSTRUCTION

This fireplace may be constructed with a slightly raised hearth, as shown in figure 3, or the hearth may be practically level with the surface of the surrounding ground.

The firebox is larger than the average size. The hearth is raised above the surrounding ground level, and slopes towards the front.

The solid plate is securely attached, as shown in figure 5, and the height of the firebox is approximately 9 inches.

VARIATIONS IN DESIGN

If this unit were used as a fireplace, it would seem practical to have a movable plate or a hinged plate, in which case the plate could be removed, or raised and leaned against the back of the fireplace in order to create a warming fire. In order to create a better draft a procedure is sometimes adopted whereby the back edge of the cast-iron top is turned up at an angle as shown in plate IX, although not quite as pronounced as in plate IX.

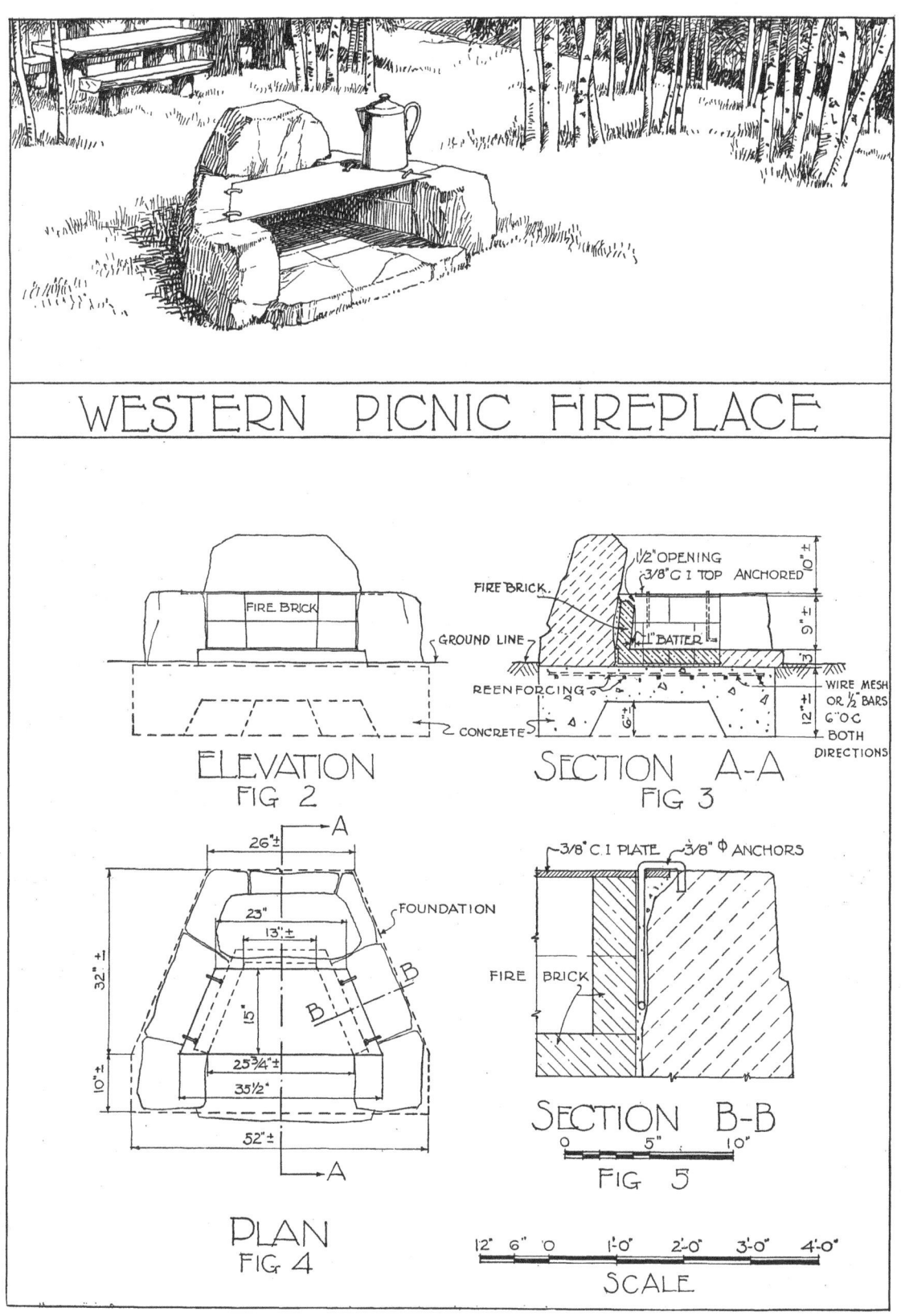

WESTERN PICNIC FIREPLACE

FIRE BRICK

ELEVATION
FIG 2

1½" OPENING
3/8" C I TOP ANCHORED
FIRE BRICK.
GROUND LINE
1" BATTER
REENFORCING
CONCRETE
WIRE MESH
OR ½ BARS
6" O C
BOTH
DIRECTIONS
10"±
9"±
3"
12"±
6"

SECTION A-A
FIG 3

26"±
23"
13"±
15"
25¾"±
35½"
52"±
32"±
10"±
A
A
FOUNDATION
B
B
B

PLAN
FIG 4

3/8" C I PLATE
3/8" Ø ANCHORS
FIRE BRICK

SECTION B-B
FIG 5
0   5"   10"

SCALE
12" 6" 0   1'-0"   2'-0"   3'-0"   4'-0"

PLATE V

INFORMAL RAISED HEARTH TYPE

ADAPTATION TO LOCATION AND USE

The adaptation to location is similar to fireplace in plate IV. This fireplace should be constructed of informal stonework in order to avoid any formal effect contrasting unnecessarily with the natural conditions. In fact it is advisable in this type with the raised hearth to do a small amount of grading at the back and sides in order to lessen the height of this structure.

The raised hearth makes it possible to develop a higher elevation for the cooking surface on the top of the grate or plate. This added height for the cooking surfaces makes the unit more convenient, and of value for camp sites as well as picnic areas.

The hinged grate and the raised back offer the opportunity to convert this fireplace into a campfire or warming fireplace, which also increases its desirability.

DESIGN AND CONSTRUCTION

This type of fireplace has the stone masonry sides, except the shoulders, level with the top of the fire-clay brick and it also has a raised back against which the hinged grate may rest. Note the suggestion for a projecting stone platform on which to set cooking utensils.

The foundation should be a reenforced floating pad as shown on figure 3.

The raised hearth is constructed of fire-clay brick laid on masonry fill on the top of the concrete pad and the appearance of this fireplace is improved by the construction of a narrow hearthstone (fig. 1) across the front.

The firebox is lined with fire-clay brick. The single rod across the front part of the firebox is used for supporting fuel in order to increase the draft when the fire is being started. The use of this bar is somewhat questionable because an accumulation of ashes would soon offset any advantage gained by the effort to provide this air space, and furthermore, the bar so buried in live coals will eventually "burn out."

The stonework is so constructed that it protects the fire-clay brick and conceals this lining to some extent as seen from the front.

The grate is hinged on a bar which is sunk into "sleeves" inserted in the stonework (pl. XXI, fig. 5, plan B).

The hinge rod (pl. XXI, figs. 2 and 3) provides a method for securely fastening the grate or plate to the fireplace in a simple and solid manner. This provision also makes it easier to remove the ashes from the firebox. The grate, as hinged, may be raised and supported against the back of the fireplace in order to create the effect of an open fire.

VARIATIONS IN DESIGN

For variations in design, refer to plate VII.

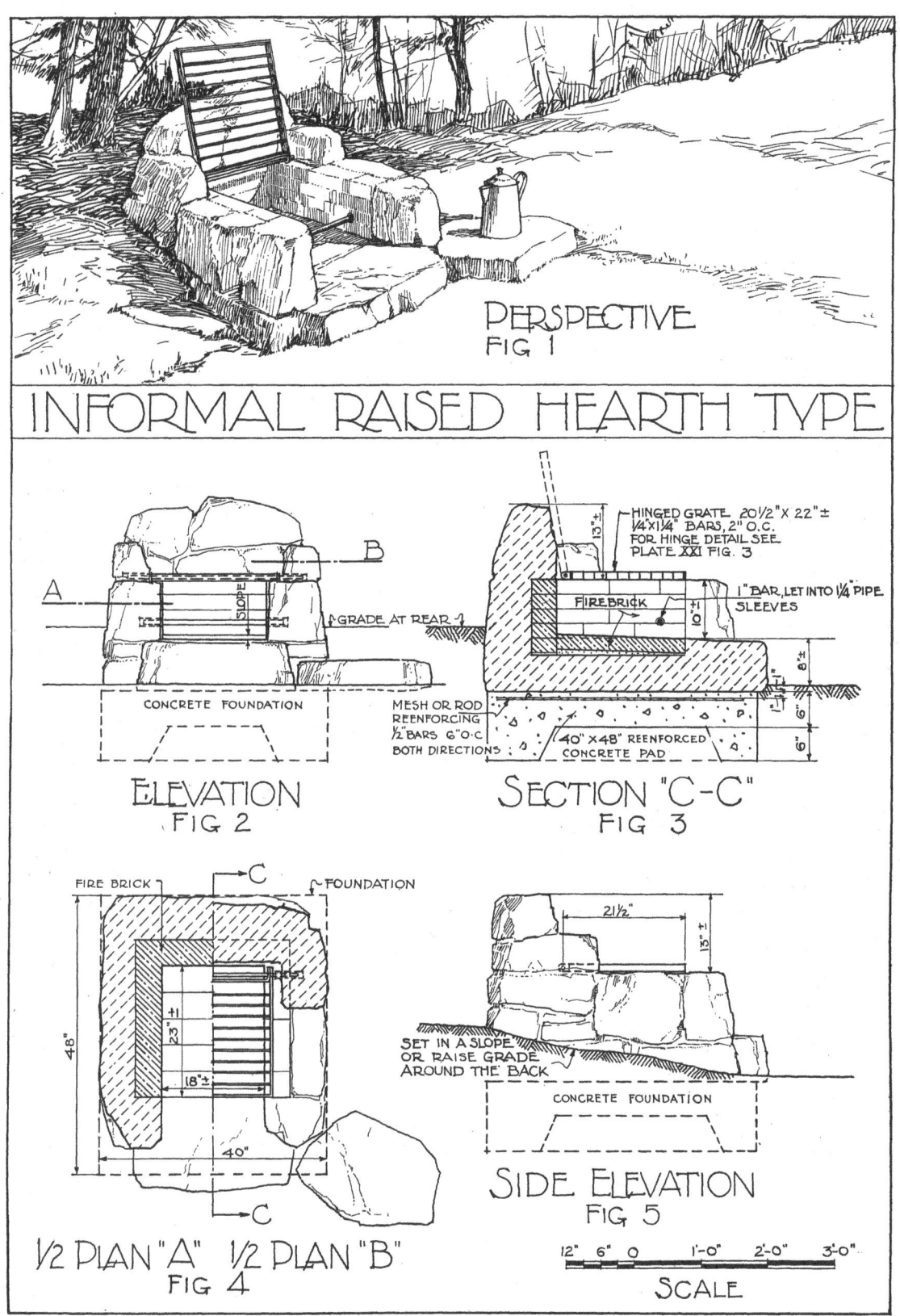

PERSPECTIVE
FIG 1

INFORMAL RAISED HEARTH TYPE

A

B

SLOPE

GRADE AT REAR

CONCRETE FOUNDATION

ELEVATION
FIG 2

HINGED GRATE 20½"X 22"±
¼"X1¼" BARS, 2" O.C.
FOR HINGE DETAIL SEE
PLATE XXI FIG. 3

13"±

FIREBRICK

1" BAR, LET INTO 1¼ PIPE
SLEEVES

10"±

8"±

MESH OR ROD
REENFORCING
½" BARS 6" O.C.
BOTH DIRECTIONS

40" X48" REENFORCED
CONCRETE PAD

6"

6"

SECTION "C-C"
FIG 3

FIRE BRICK

C

FOUNDATION

23"±

18"±

48"

40"

C

½ PLAN "A" ½ PLAN "B"
FIG 4

21½"

15"±

SET IN A SLOPE
OR RAISE GRADE
AROUND THE BACK

CONCRETE FOUNDATION

SIDE ELEVATION
FIG 5

12" 6" 0   1'-0"   2'-0"   3'-0"

SCALE

PLATE VI

37

INFORMAL RAISED HEARTH TYPE

ADAPTATION TO LOCATION AND USE

This type has the same problems concerning adaptations to location and to use as relate to the fireplace shown in plate VI.

DESIGN AND CONSTRUCTION

The slabs of stone on which to set cooking utensils, and related to the fireplace as indicated in the sketch, have a tendency to more directly "tie" this feature to the ground. The single capstone across the back of the fireplace extends over and is set flush with the face of the fire-clay brick lining in order to improve the design and the construction. The front corners of the fireplace are returned in such a manner that they partially conceal the fire-clay brick lining.

The hearth if raised to a height approximately 12 inches above the ground level, would bring the cooking surface at the top of the grate or plate to a height of 22 inches, which would make the unit more convenient for camp use, and more massive.

This entire structure (excepting the single slabs of rock at either side) should rest upon a reenforced concrete floating pad foundation. The flanking rocks are buried slightly in the ground.

The hearth should be constructed of fire-clay brick laid on a masonry fill on top of the concrete foundation. There may or may not be a projecting stone hearth at the front of the fireplace.

The fire-clay brick is anchored by the cap stone across the back and is carried only to the level of the stone masonry wall on the sides. In this method of construction, the joint between the fire-clay brick and the stonework should be very carefully constructed in order to avoid the possibility of water entering between the fire-clay brick and the stonework, thus causing damage during the winter months.

The success of this fireplace depends upon the use of large units of stone of a uniform character, and upon a careful treatment of the joints in order to conceal them as much as possible. The flanking rocks which are not set upon any foundation should be entirely free from the fireplace structure, so that in heaving and settling under frost action no damage will be done to the stone masonry.

VARIATION IN DESIGN

A variation (figs. 2 and 6) indicates the hearth lowered to the ground level with the fire-clay brick in the hearth omitted, and sand or mineral earth substituted in its place. In this variation in design the foundations under the side and rear walls should be carried below the frost line.

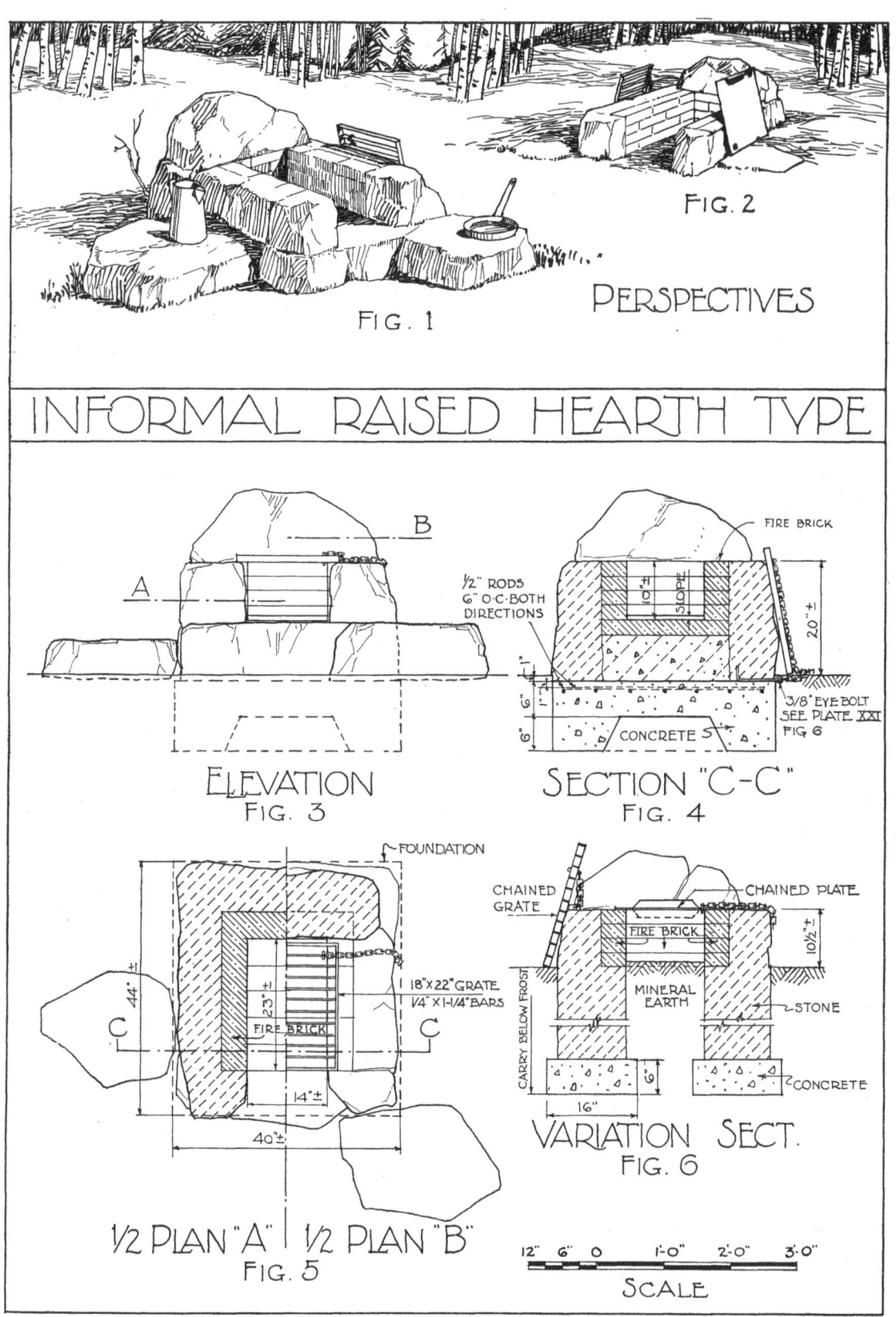

FIG. 2

PERSPECTIVES

FIG. 1

INFORMAL RAISED HEARTH TYPE

B

A

ELEVATION
FIG. 3

FIRE BRICK

½" RODS
6" O·C·BOTH
DIRECTIONS

HOT SLOPE

2'-0"±

3/8" EYE BOLT
SEE PLATE XXI
FIG 6

CONCRETE

SECTION "C-C"
FIG. 4

FOUNDATION

44"±

C   C

23"±

FIRE BRICK

18"x 22" GRATE
¼"X 1-¼" BARS

14"±

40"±

½ PLAN "A" | ½ PLAN "B"
FIG. 5

CHAINED
GRATE

CHAINED PLATE

FIRE BRICK

10½"±

CARRY BELOW FROST

MINERAL
EARTH

STONE

6"

16"

CONCRETE

VARIATION SECT.
FIG. 6

12" 6" 0   1'-0"   2'-0"   3'-0"

SCALE

PLATE VII

39

CHIMNEY NOTCH TYPE

ADAPTATION TO LOCATION AND USE

Because of the raised back and the chimney notch effect which takes the place of a chimney, when a solid plate is used for the top, it is essential that this fireplace, so far as is practical, be oriented to take advantage of the prevailing wind.

This fireplace, especially with the solid plate, is adapted for use on campgrounds, especially if the hearth is raised to make the top of the plate approximately 14 to 16 inches above the ground.

This type is a "cross" between an open fireplace with a solid back (pl. VII) and the low chimney type (pl. X). Its distinct advantage is that it is easily converted from a fairly efficient cooking fireplace with an iron plate cooking surface, into an open reflecting fireplace for campfire use in the evening.

DESIGN AND CONSTRUCTION

Converting this unit from a cooking fireplace to a campfire is accomplished by tilting the top plate against the notch with the narrow side resting on the hearth at the back of the firebox, as shown in figure 2.

The dimensions of the firebox and of the top plate are so related that the plate when stood on its narrow side will easily fit into the firebox as shown in figure 2. The depth of the firebox from front to back should be 2 inches less than the width. In order to have the plate set on the top of the fire-clay brick lining, the plate should be 4 inches longer than the width of the firebox, thus allowing a 2-inch overlap on each end of the plate. In this instance, the width of the firebox is 16 inches and the depth of the firebox is 14 inches. The length of the plate is 20 inches and the width of the plate is 14 inches.

This structure is also supported on a reenforced concrete floating pad. The hearth is constructed of fire-clay brick, and the firebox is lined with fire-clay brick, including the chimney notch. The stonework partially conceals the fire-clay brick, as shown in the drawing.

The grate or plate should be removable, with the flange on the front edge of the plate turned down, and the flange on the rear edge turned up, and it should be attached by a chain to the stonework. The bent flanges will tend to prevent sagging. (See pl. XXII, fig. 4.)

VARIATIONS IN DESIGN

The only variation in design which seems of sufficient importance is the raising of the hearth where this unit is used primarily for campgrounds.

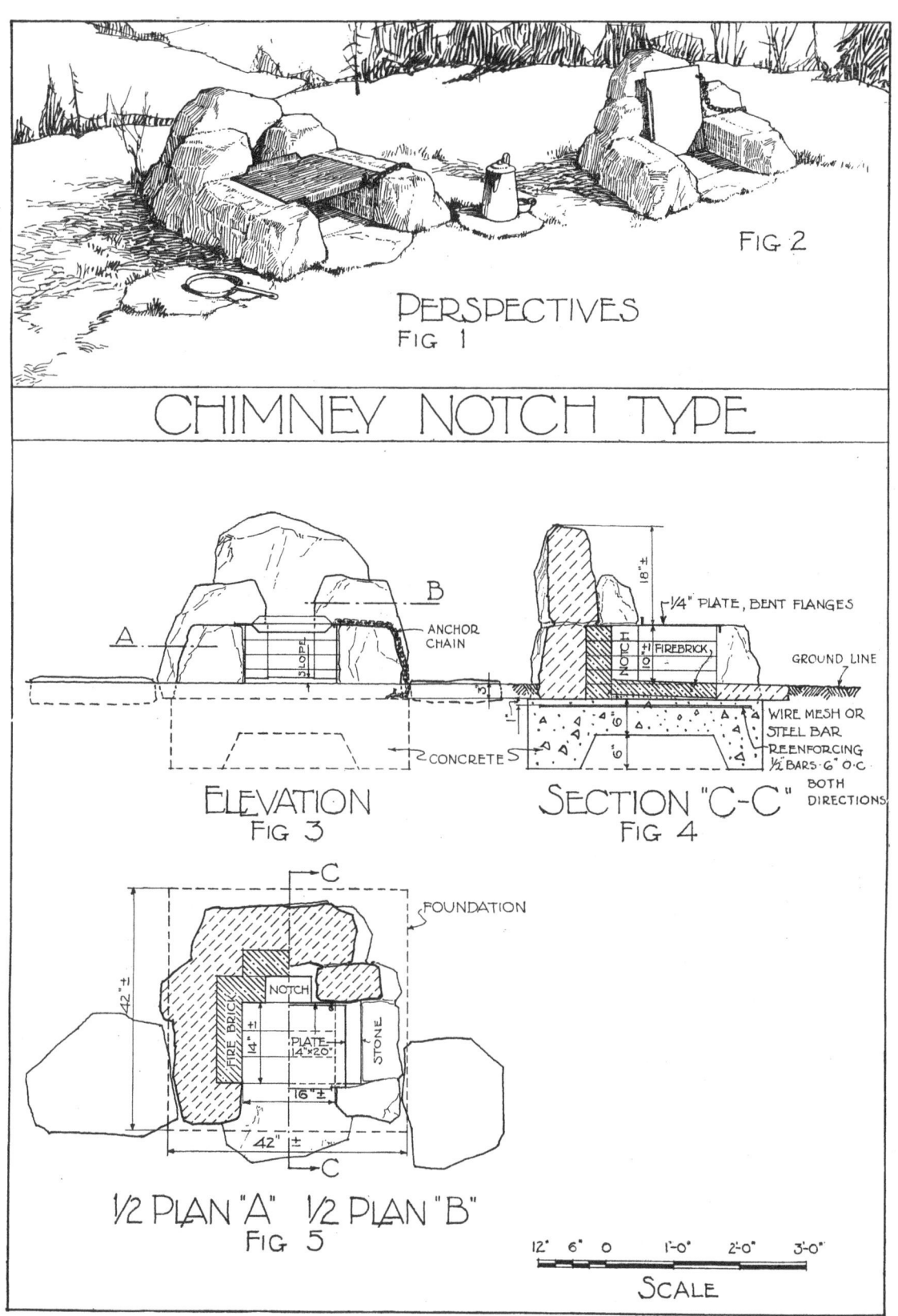

PERSPECTIVES
FIG 1

FIG 2

CHIMNEY NOTCH TYPE

ELEVATION
FIG 3

SECTION "C-C"
FIG 4

½ PLAN "A"   ½ PLAN "B"
FIG 5

SCALE

12" 6" 0   1'-0"   2'-0"   3'-0"

PLATE VIII

CONVERTIBLE CAMP STOVE

ADAPTATION TO LOCATION AND USE

This camp stove is an unusual type, the fundamental idea for which was developed by region 1 of the United States Forest Service. It is especially well adapted for use in the forest areas, where camp stove cooking facilities are required. The unit is low and, if carefully constructed with an appropriate type of stone found in the immediate locality, this stove is most acceptable.

The necessity for a chimney, which adds to the massiveness of any camp stove, is avoided by the hinged plate shown in figure 4. In the areas of high fire hazard, it is difficult in this stove to control the sparks, which in the type shown on plate X can be easily controlled by a spark arrester in the low chimney.

This stove is easily converted into a warming fire by raising the plate, as shown in figures 2 and 4.

Most camp stoves are too massive for use in open and semiopen areas, and are only adapted for practical use in connection with camp units where natural screen planting between the units exists. The necessity for screen planting where this stove is used is not as great as where the larger and more imposing units are used. This type of camp stove seems to have excellent possibilities as a most useful unit easily converted from picnic use to camp use or vice versa.

DESIGN AND CONSTRUCTION

The plate may be of cast iron or of 10-gage boilerplate, bent to fit the design of the stove as shown in figures 1 and 4. If a cast-iron plate is used, the front part of the plate should be counterbalanced by additional weight in the curved portion of the plate back of the hinge in order that the sudden dropping of the plate on the top of the brickwork will not injure the plate. If 10-gage boiler plate is used for the top of the fireplace, it is not necessary that any counterbalance weight be used.

The hinge on which the plate revolves is located as shown in figure 4 and is anchored in the stone masonry as shown in figure 6. The increased width of the front portion of the plate (figs. 1 and 5) allows the plate when raised to rest against the side walls, as shown in figure 2.

The hearth should slope slightly to the front, and at the front edge it may be level with the surrounding ground. If, in exceptional instances, the camper desires a more convenient height for the top of the plate, the hearth may be raised approximately 6 inches above the ground level.

The underside of the plate is reenforced with 2- by 2-inch angle irons, which are welded to the plate to prevent warping and possible sagging. These angles are pierced to allow the hinge rod to pass through.

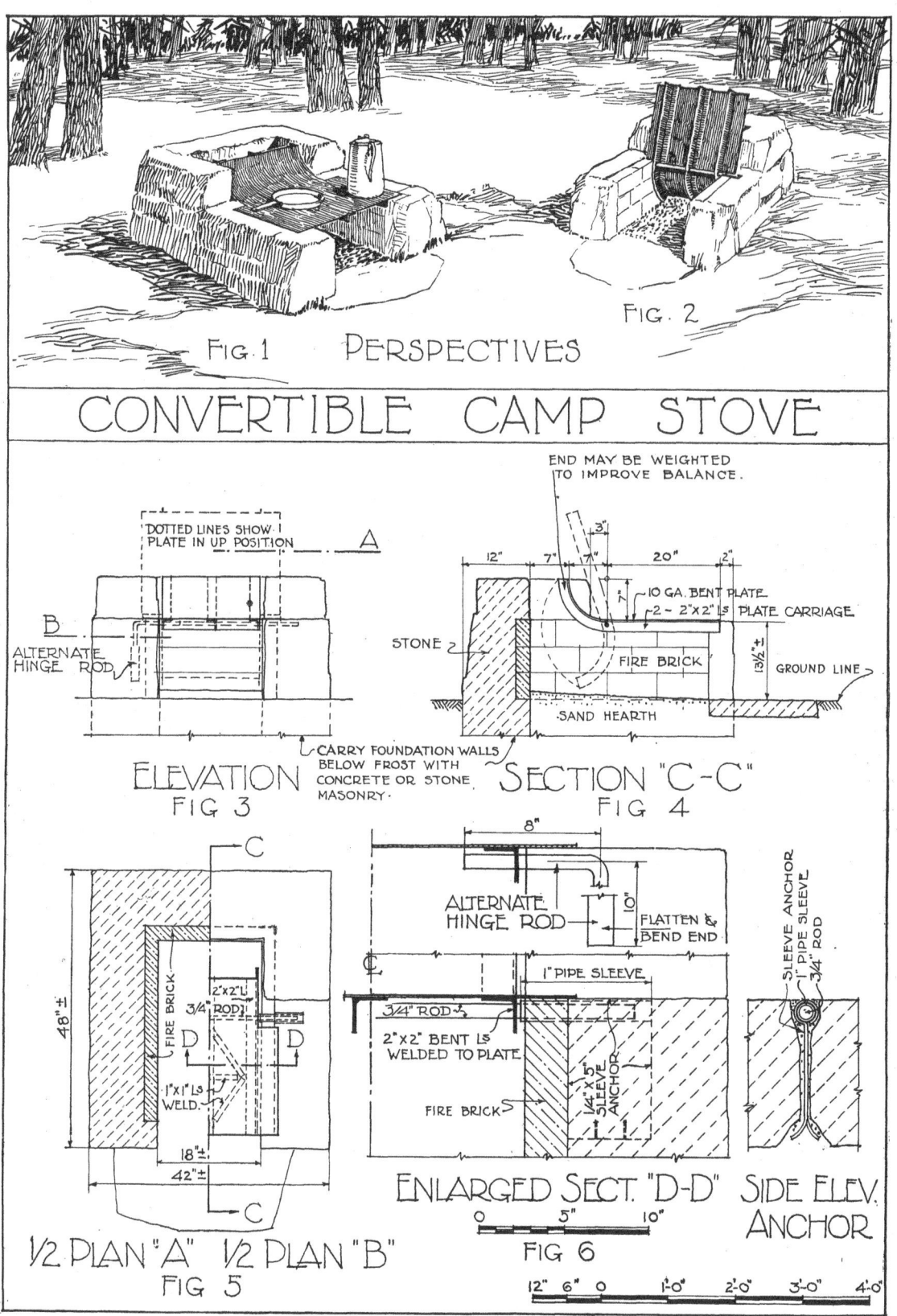

FIG. 1   PERSPECTIVES   FIG. 2

CONVERTIBLE CAMP STOVE

ELEVATION
FIG 3

SECTION "C-C"
FIG 4

½ PLAN "A" ½ PLAN "B"
FIG 5

ENLARGED SECT. "D-D"   SIDE ELEV.
FIG 6   ANCHOR

PLATE IX

43

STOVE-WARMING COMBINATION

ADAPTATION TO LOCATION AND USE

This fireplace approaches the camp stove type and is excellently adapted to campground use. These larger types are not recommended for the open and extensive picnic areas requiring a number of cooking units. The ideal location for such fireplaces is one where the ground level may be raised at the sides and the back to reduce apparent height.

The low chimney in which a spark arrester may be inserted, if necessary, is added protection against any fire hazard, especially in the timber areas of the West.

The use of this unit as a cooking stove, or as a warming fire, is easily accomplished by raising the hinged plate and the grill as shown in figure 4.

DESIGN AND CONSTRUCTION

The design includes provision for a grill or grate and/or a solid plate, both of which are hinged on bar hinges as shown in plate XXI, figure 4. When the top grate and plate are thrown back against the chimney, this unit is converted into a warming fireplace. For use in cooking, either the grill or the plate may be used.

Where fuel economy is an important factor, the shelf shown in figures 4 and 5 may be lengthened as indicated by the dotted lines, thus reducing the depth of the firebox proper while retaining the same area of cooking surface.

The stone platforms on which to place cooking utensils may be constructed as shown in the sketch.

The foundation for this type of fireplace should be carried below the frost line and the fire-clay brick hearth should be supported on a reenforced concrete slab, as shown on this drawing. The firebox is lined with fire-clay brick laid as stretchers. The top plate ought to be 10-gage sheet iron. It is not necessary to reenforce this plate because the plate will rest directly on top of the grate.

The stonework must be laid in an informal manner with carefully selected native stove.

The low chimney is lined with fire-clay brick, laid flatwise. An arch constructed of fire-clay brick extends across the flue opening. The top of this arched opening is slightly below the level of the plate.

VARIATIONS IN DESIGN

Where steelwork is available at no abnormal cost, two 3- by 3-inch angles with 1/4- by 9-inch plate riveted to the under side may replace the arch and will improve the appearance.

The raised hearth may be omitted if the lower elevation of the top is acceptable and the height of the entire mass will thus be reduced approximately 8 inches.

44

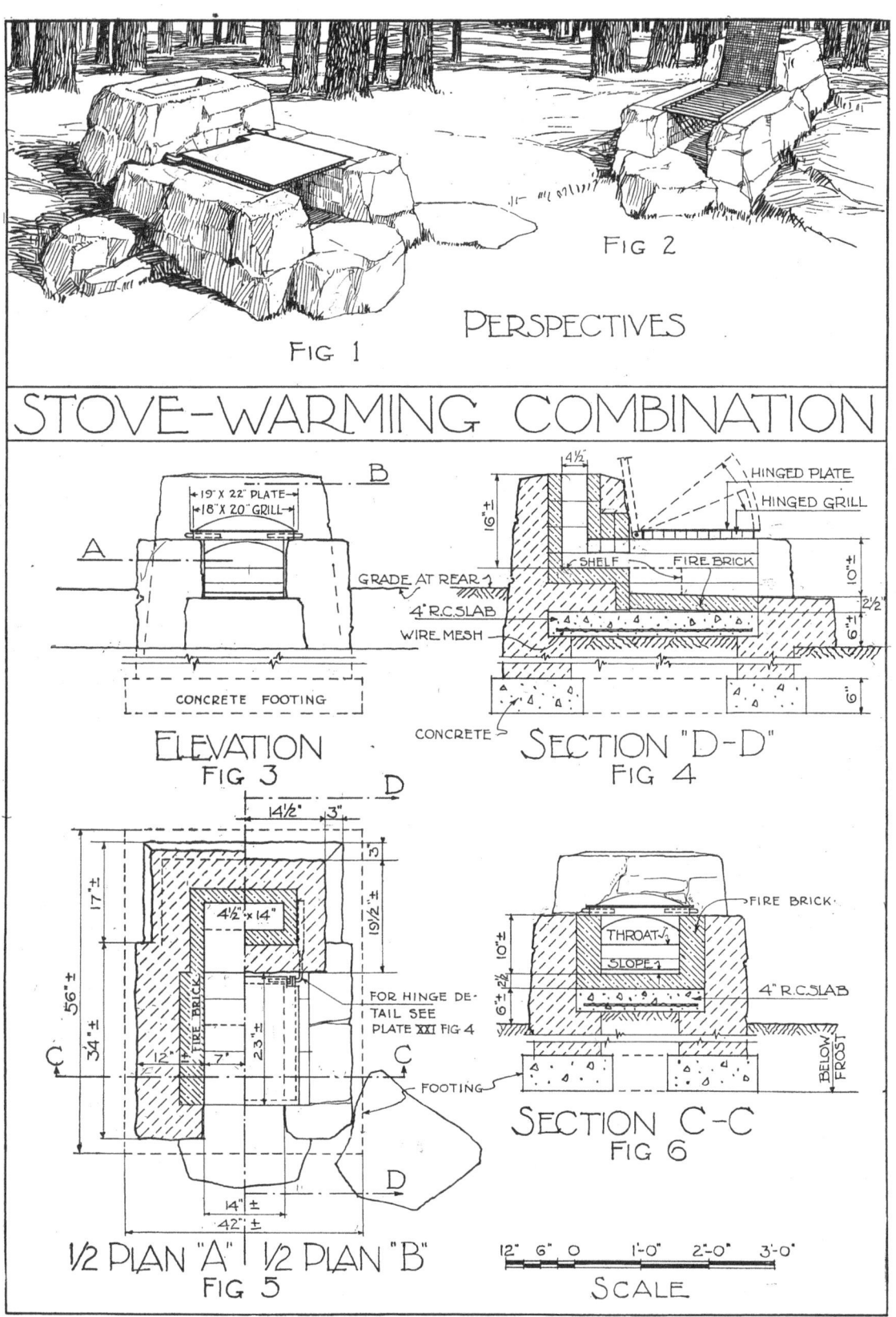

FIG 2

PERSPECTIVES

FIG 1

STOVE-WARMING COMBINATION

B

19" X 22" PLATE
18" X 20" GRILL

A

ELEVATION
FIG 3

CONCRETE FOOTING

4½

HINGED PLATE
HINGED GRILL

16"±

SHELF   FIRE BRICK

10"±

GRADE AT REAR

4" R.C.SLAB

WIRE MESH

2½

6"±

CONCRETE

SECTION "D-D"
FIG 4

6"

D

14½"   3"

3

17"±

4½" X 14"

19½"±

56"±

FIRE BRICK

FOR HINGE DE-
TAIL SEE
PLATE XXI FIG 4

34"±

2-3"±

1½   7"

C   C

FOOTING

D

14"±

42"±

½ PLAN "A"   ½ PLAN "B"
FIG 5

FIRE BRICK

THROAT
SLOPE

4" R.C.SLAB

10"±

6"± 2½

BELOW
FROST

SECTION C-C
FIG 6

12" 6" O   1'-0"   2'-0"   3'-0"

SCALE

PLATE X

CONVERTIBLE CAMP STOVE

ADAPTATION TO LOCATION AND USE

This type is primarily a camp stove, although it may be used as a campfire. The simpler units (pls. IV, V, and VIII) are appropriate for the natural forest areas. There is, however, in many campgrounds, especially in the larger timber, a definite need for this convertible unit which eliminates undue fire hazard, provides for cooking and for warming fire use, and increases the convenience of everyday use in a camp.

These units ought to be so located that a screen of natural growth will separate one from the other.

This camp stove, together with the stove shown in plate XI–A, figure 4, are excellently adapted to campground use.

DESIGN AND CONSTRUCTION

It should be constructed with an interesting texture of informal stonework and should tie naturally to the surrounding ground.

In addition to the sand or gravel area which naturally should surround any campfire or camp-stove unit, there might well be a few flagstones immediately in front of this camp stove.

The foundation walls should extend below frost, in order to avoid the danger of uneven settlement due to the excess of weight at the chimney end of the camp stove.

The chimney is lined with fire-clay brick and the firebox is lined to the height of the side walls. The firebox is entirely enclosed by the solid top plate and the single door or double doors across the front.

The solid top plate extends 2 inches over the brickwork on either side and it is hinged at the rear of the firebox as shown in figure 2. In order to convert this stove into a campfire, the doors are opened and the top is thrown back against the chimney. A certain amount of heat will continue to go up the chimney unless a damper is installed to control the draft.

The danger of warping is decreased by the welding of two 1 by 1 inch angles across the underside of the top plate (pl. XXII, fig. 4).

The chimney approximates $3\frac{1}{2}$ feet in height above ground level. It may be lined with lava rock, or it may have a terra-cotta flue lining in place of the fire-clay brick. It is very desirable that a spark arrester be inserted in the top of the chimney, especially if the fire hazard is very great.

VARIATIONS IN DESIGN

It is entirely practical to have the firebox with the sides parallel (pl. XI–A, fig. 4), rather than to have the front of the firebox wider than the rear, although the splayed sides reflect more heat when used as a warming fire.

If the front doors are omitted, then it will be necessary to install a damper in the chimney in order to properly control the draft.

In figure 4, the height of the top plate above the ground is approximately 16 inches. This top plate may be lowered approximately 4 inches by omitting the raised hearth and thus leaving a total height of approximately 12 inches between the surface of the ground and the top of the plate, with chimney lowered proportionately.

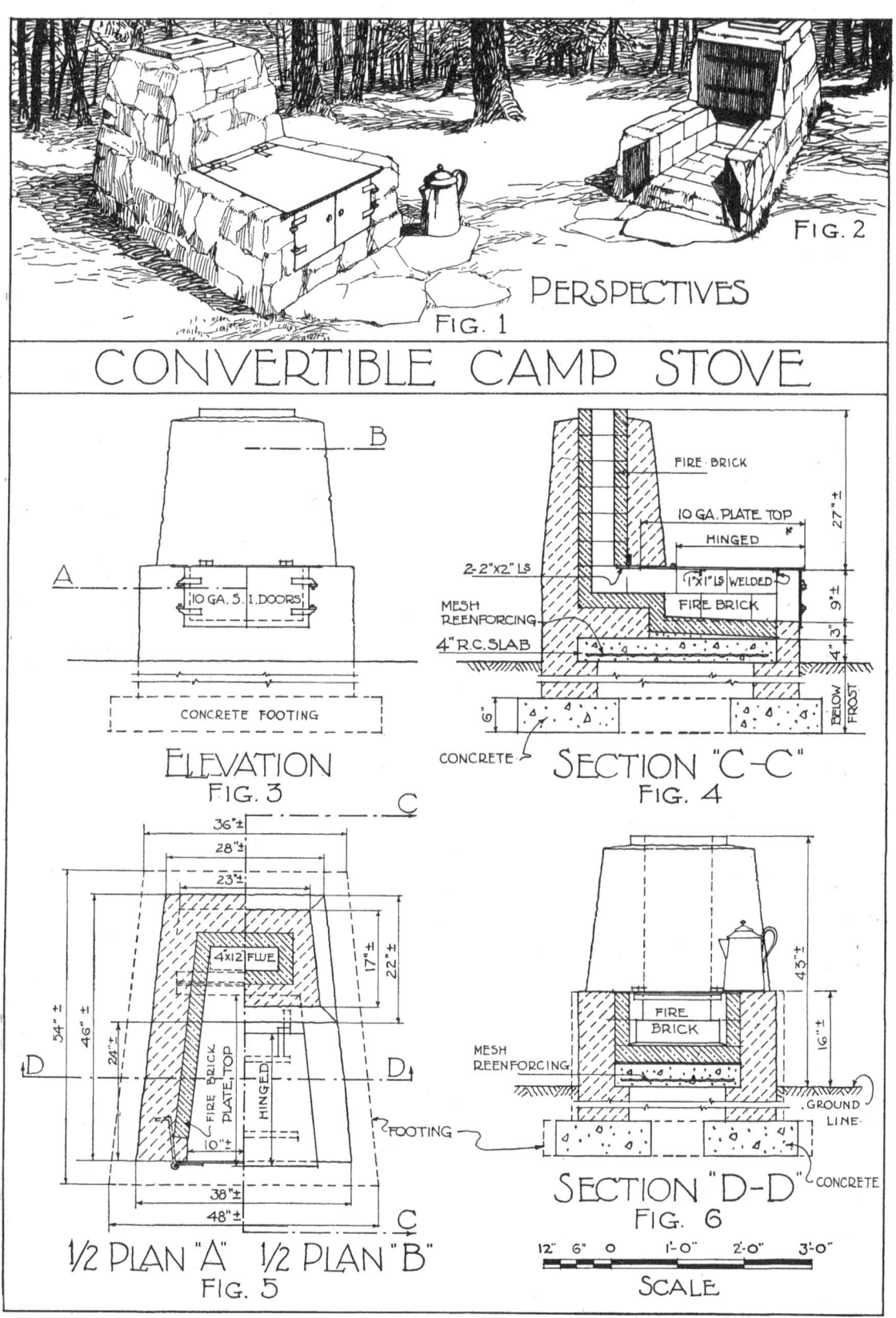

PERSPECTIVES

FIG. 2

FIG. 1

CONVERTIBLE CAMP STOVE

B

A

10 GA. S. I. DOORS

CONCRETE FOOTING

ELEVATION
FIG. 3

FIRE BRICK

10 GA. PLATE TOP

HINGED

2-2"x2" LS

1"x1" LS WELDED

FIRE BRICK

MESH REENFORCING

4" R.C. SLAB

27"±

9"±

3"

4"

6"

BELOW FROST

CONCRETE

SECTION "C-C"
FIG. 4

C

36"±

28"±

23"±

17"±

22"±

4x12 FLUE

FIRE BRICK PLATE TOP

HINGED

54"±

46"±

24"±

10"±

38"±

48"±

D

D

C

½ PLAN "A"   ½ PLAN "B"
FIG. 5

FIRE BRICK

MESH REENFORCING

FOOTING

45"±

16"±

GROUND LINE

CONCRETE

SECTION "D-D"
FIG. 6

12" 6" 0   1'-0"   2'-0"   3'-0"

SCALE

PLATE XI

CAMP STOVE VARIATIONS

UPON this plate there are shown a few variations of camp-stove designs some of which are excellent for certain uses and some of which do not seem to be practical except under conditions which impose unusual requirements upon the camp-stove design.

The details for design of these stoves are not covered in a special drawing because those desirable features are covered directly or in modified form by parts of drawings on other plates.

Each of these variations in type is discussed under its individual heading.

The desirable stoves for campground use are those shown in plates III–A, VII, VIII, IX, X, and XI, or variations of some of these types. Figures 3 and 4 in plate XI–A especially when providing for a combination top grate and top plate may be adapted for use as a fireplace or as a camp stove.

CAMP STOVE WITH GRATE AND SLIDING TOP PLATE

The usual method of designing combination op grate and top plate is as shown in plate X or as is shown in plate VII. In the first instance the plate is hinged over the grate and in the second instance the plate is removable.

Figure 1 shows a suggested method of providing a sliding plate which may be pulled to one side as shown in the drawing, thus exposing the grate for broiling and grilling.

This type of design is not simple. Such stoves are expensive to construct. The top plate if too thick decreases the heating efficiency to a very marked extent. This stove does not seem to have a definite place for campground use in the forests and is therefore not recommended.

CAMP STOVE WITH ASHPIT AREA IN FRONT OF FIREBOX

This type of stove is similar in design to the stove shown in figure 4 with the exception that the shallow enclosed pit in front of the firebox is added to this unit to serve a dual purpose as follows:

(a) To be used as an ashpit in areas where there is abnormal fire hazard. (There seem to be very few areas where this abnormal precaution is necessary especially if a hearth of flagstone or mineral earth is provided immediately in front of the firebox.)

(b) To provide a space into which to pull the live coals so that a toaster or a grill may be placed across the top on which to broil steak and other meats.

This added feature constructed as shown in figure 2 makes an abnormally long unit of a camp stove. This ashpit area is in no way essential if the combination grate and plate is used for the top.

CAMP STOVE WITH GRATE IN BOTTOM OF FIREBOX

In some areas where a condition of excessive moisture (rain or fog) prevails it is sometimes desirable to so construct the camp stove that a bottom draft may be procured through a grate in the bottom of the firebox. Such a type of design is not generally recommended except where the condition of the wood used for fuel is so affected by the moisture that this additional bottom draft is necessary.

CAMP STOVE WITH SOLID TOP PLATE

One of the most practical camp stoves is that shown in figure 4. The efficiency of this stove might be much increased if it were so designed that a combination grate and plate properly hinged as shown in plate X were used. The solid plate on the top of this stove does not permit any use for broiling over a grate and neither does it provide opportunity for use as a fireplace with the top plate raised as shown in plate XI, figure 2. It is also desirable in these camp stoves to provide a damper preferably in the chimney as shown in plate XI–A, figure 5.

48

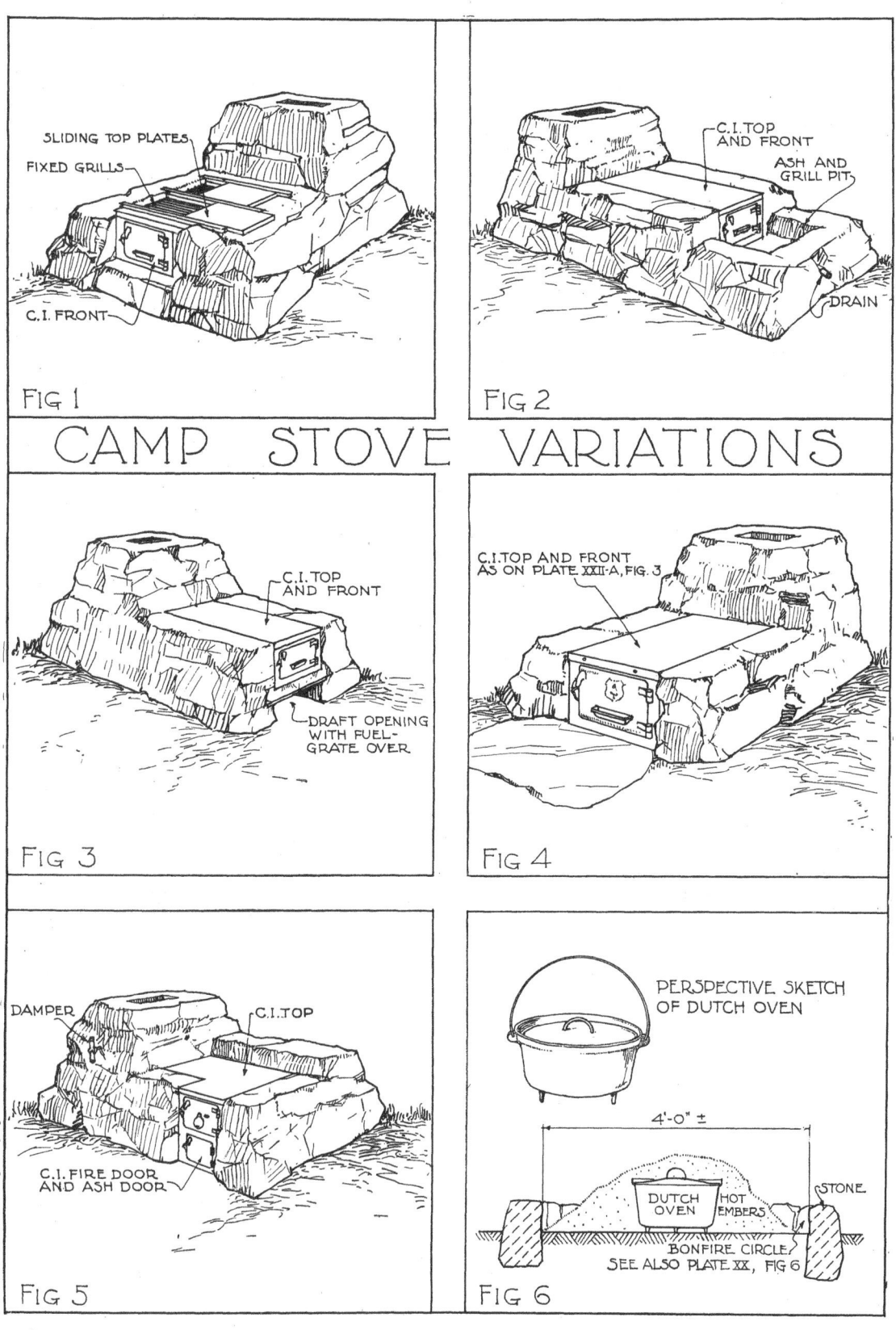

FIG 1

SLIDING TOP PLATES
FIXED GRILLS
C.I. FRONT

FIG 2

C.I. TOP AND FRONT
ASH AND GRILL PIT
DRAIN

CAMP STOVE VARIATIONS

FIG 3

C.I. TOP AND FRONT
DRAFT OPENING WITH FUEL-GRATE OVER

FIG 4

C.I. TOP AND FRONT AS ON PLATE XXII-A, FIG. 3

FIG 5

DAMPER
C.I. TOP
C.I. FIRE DOOR AND ASH DOOR

FIG 6

PERSPECTIVE SKETCH OF DUTCH OVEN

4'-0" ±

DUTCH OVEN   HOT EMBERS
STONE
BONFIRE CIRCLE
SEE ALSO PLATE XX, FIG 6

PLATE XI-A

49

CAMP STOVES WITH THE DOOR ON THE SIDE

In some campgrounds it seems desirable to adopt a type of camp stove such as is shown in plate XI–A, figure 5. The advantages claimed for this stove are the following:

(a) An economy of fuel because the firebox is very small in proportion to the cooking area on the top of the stove. The heat under a portion of the top plate is produced by the flames which travel under this plate to the flue, in which a damper is constructed.

(b) A cooking ledge is provided on the front of the stove to be used for warming purposes.

(c) A "windbreak wall" may be constructed on the windward side to protect the top from any abnormal currents of air caused by prevailing winds, especially in the higher mountain country where a strong wind generally prevails, especially in the late fall and early spring.

This stove, if well constructed and kept sufficiently low by eliminating the ashpit under the firebox, is an appropriate unit in the forest surroundings. It is undoubtedly more expensive to construct than the more simple type of stove shown in figure 4.

DUTCH OVENS

The dutch oven is probably one of the simplest and most effective method of cooking certain foods.

In areas of considerable fire hazard and especially in the primitive areas, it is desirable to construct a small pit, similar to a campfire circle, surrounded by a row of stones which will confine the fire within a specific area.

The success with which a dutch oven may be used for cooking depends very largely upon the experience and ability of the person who is using the oven. The general method of using this oven is that of building a fire in a small campfire circle (fig. 6). After this fire has burned sufficiently long to produce a liberal bed of live coals, these coals are so arranged that the dutch oven, containing the meat or other food to be cooked, can be set firmly into the bed of coals. After the cover has been securely fastened, the entire dutch oven is completely covered (fig. 6) with coals and left thus buried in a bed of coals and ashes for the length of time necessary to properly cook the meat or other food to be placed in the oven.

HIGH CHIMNEY STOVE

ADAPTATION TO LOCATION AND USE

The high chimney stove has little or no place in the national forest areas, because of its massiveness. The discussion covering camp stoves would not be complete without including this type of stove because, in a few locations where the fire hazard is abnormally high and where it is possible to provide an adequate screen between the different camp units, such a stove might be used. Its general use should be discouraged.

The cost of constructing such a unit seems to be out of proportion to the results which are obtained, as compared with the results that can be obtained in the construction of the simpler types of definite camp stoves shown particularly in plates IX, X, XI, and XI–A, figure 4.

This feature more nearly approaches the conveniences of the stove at home and, for this reason alone, it deprives one of some of the satisfactions which come from a new kind of recreational activity in the natural out-of-doors.

DESIGN AND CONSTRUCTION

This unit becomes increasingly objectionable unless the stone used in its construction is carefully selected and equally carefully laid, in order to avoid some of the objectionable textures of stonework illustrated in plates XXIV and XXV.

The foundation on which this stove rests should be carried below the frost line, as shown in figure 4, and it may be constructed by placing rocks in the concrete to lessen the amount of concrete required.

The stove is provided with a definite firebox and an ashpit, separated with a grate. The draft is controlled by a damper in the chimney and oftentimes by a damper in the door at the front of the firebox. The doors and the top plate are generally made of cast iron.

As shown in the drawings, the firebox and the flue should be carefully lined with fire-clay brick or other equally acceptable material.

The author has observed some of these stoves, in which the space between the back of the fire-clay brick lining and the stone masonry is left as an air space or is filled with asbestos. The author questions the necessity for this provision in the design of this type of camp stove. In any event, the top of this space should be thoroughly sealed to prevent the entrance of water.

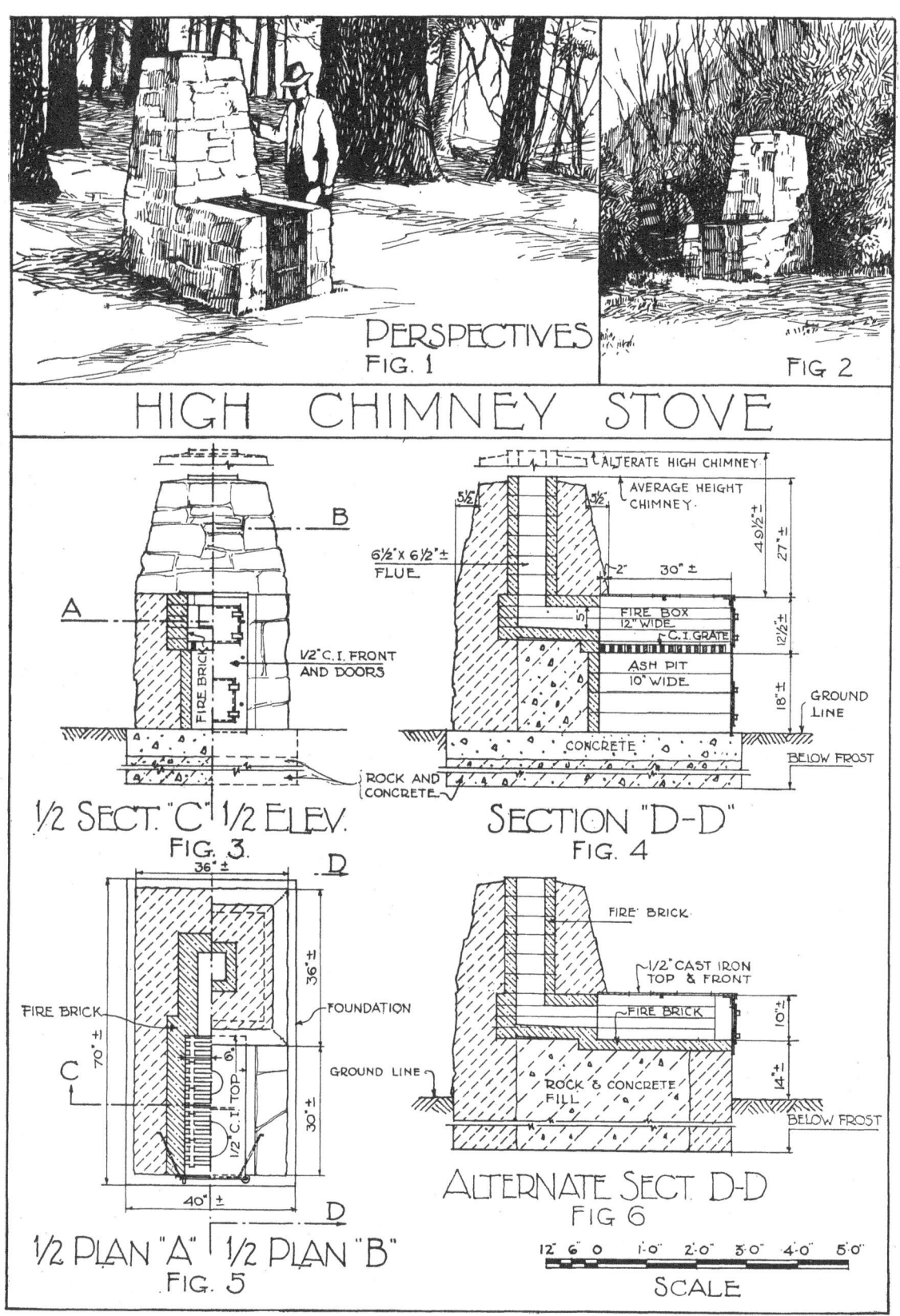

PERSPECTIVES
FIG. 1

FIG 2

HIGH CHIMNEY STOVE

B

A

FIRE BRICK

1/2" C.I. FRONT
AND DOORS

1/2 SECT. "C" 1/2 ELEV.
FIG. 3.

ROCK AND
CONCRETE

ALTERATE HIGH CHIMNEY

AVERAGE HEIGHT
CHIMNEY.

6 1/2" x 6 1/2" ±
FLUE

5 1/2

5 1/2

49 1/2" ±

27" ±

2"

30" ±

FIRE BOX
12" WIDE

C. I. GRATE

ASH PIT
10" WIDE

12 1/2" ±

18" ±

GROUND
LINE

CONCRETE

BELOW FROST

SECTION "D-D"
FIG. 4

36" ±

D

FIRE BRICK

FOUNDATION

36" ±

70" ±

6"

1/2 C.I. TOP

GROUND LINE

30" ±

40" ±

D

1/2 PLAN "A" | 1/2 PLAN "B"
FIG. 5

FIRE BRICK

1/2" CAST IRON
TOP & FRONT

FIRE BRICK

ROCK & CONCRETE
FILL

10" ±

14" ±

BELOW FROST

ALTERNATE SECT. D-D
FIG 6

12" 6" 0   1'-0"   2'-0"   3'-0"   4'-0"   5'-0"

SCALE

PLATE XII

MULTIPLE UNIT STOVE

ADAPTATION TO LOCATION AND USE

The multiple unit is a massive structure which has, with rare exceptions, no reason for existence on a national forest, and is in reality a camp stove adapted only to picnic area use. This type of multiple unit is of greatest value in connection with areas used intensively and by large organized picnic groups. It has little value on areas used for small family picnics, or on campgrounds.

It may be used in multiples of two, three, or four, as shown in figure 1. The most practical design is in multiples of two, which greatly reduces the congestion around the cooking space.

It is very seldom that a multiple unit of this kind would be used by campers, except those who live at resorts, in connection with which there are small cabins constructed close together.

This type of stove in multiple units is excellently adapted to some of the areas where there is intensive activity in winter sports.

DESIGN AND CONSTRUCTION

The foundation under these structures should extend below the frost line and the hearth should rest on a masonry fill. The hearth and the firebox should be paved with fire-clay brick.

The efficient design of these units requires a minimum length for the firebox, and a narrow entrance to the flue, creating a considerable additional warming area, as shown in figure 3. Under this type of design, the flames and the hot gases are forced through the narrow passage over the shelf which is directly under the cooking top, thus making the entire surface of the cooking top available for use.

In this drawing, a 10-gage iron top is indicated, reenforced with 1 by 1 inch angle irons welded to the undersurface as shown. The use of a thinner gage may cause buckling and sagging, and to date the information concerning this problem is not sufficiently adequate to determine the result which would occur by using any thinner material.

The high chimney may have a terra cotta flue lining, although fire-clay brick will serve equally well. Sometimes the single flue is made sufficiently large to meet the requirements of the multiple units which it serves and it should then be divided into the required number of smaller flues of the proper size. This encourages a more efficient operation by shutting out the cold air which would otherwise be drawn from the stoves not in operation.

VARIATIONS IN DESIGN

Sometimes an ash pit may be constructed under the firebox, as indicated in figure 5 and as shown in plate XII, figure 4.

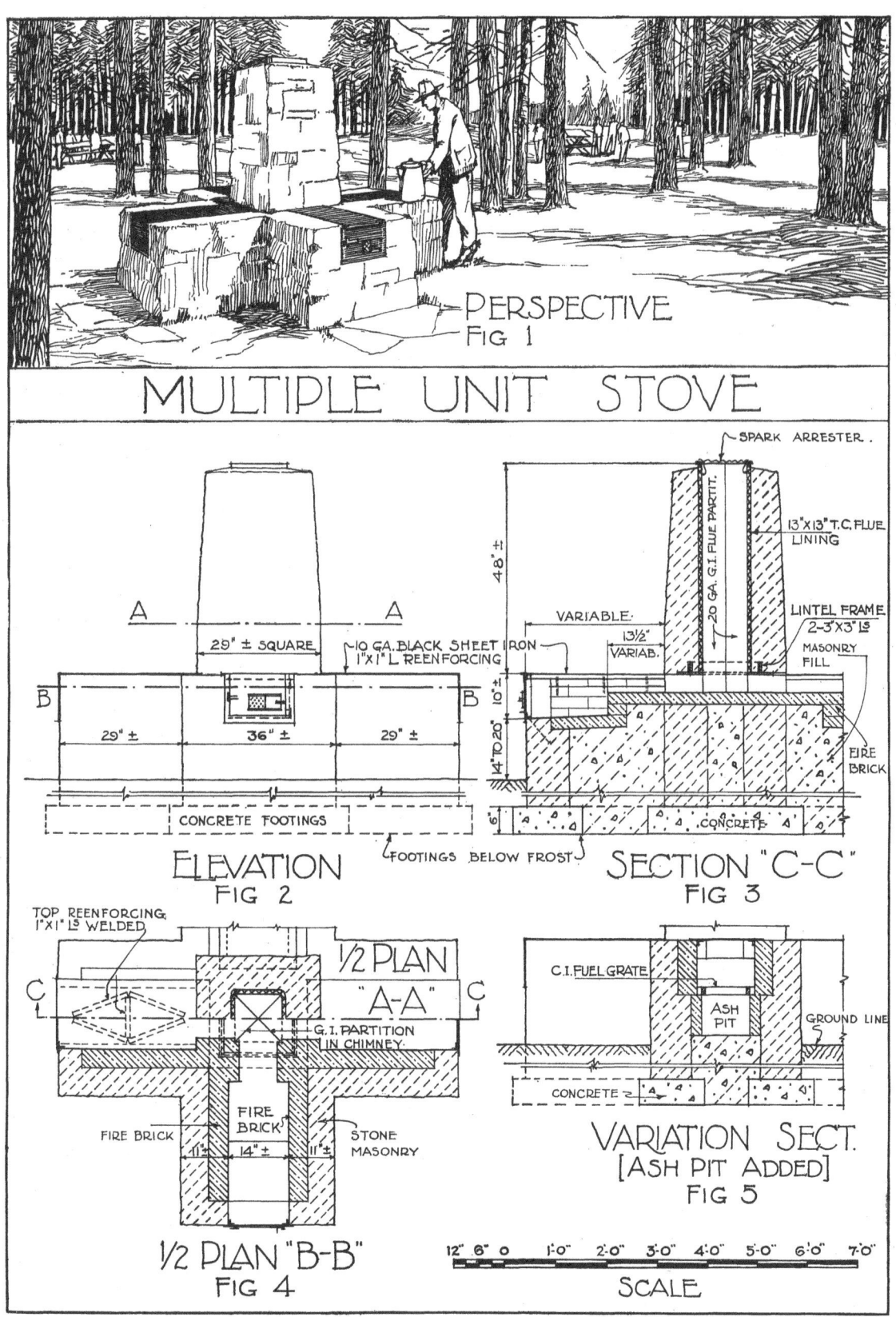

PERSPECTIVE
Fig 1

MULTIPLE UNIT STOVE

29" ± SQUARE

─10 GA. BLACK SHEET IRON
1"x1" L REENFORCING

A ─── A

B ─── B

29" ±   36" ±   29" ±

CONCRETE FOOTINGS

ELEVATION
FIG 2

FOOTINGS BELOW FROST

SPARK ARRESTER.

48" ±

VARIABLE.

13½"
VARIAB.

20 GA. G.I. FLUE PARTIT.

13"x13" T.C. FLUE
LINING

LINTEL FRAME
2-3"x3" Ls

MASONRY
FILL

10" ±

14 TO 20"

6"

CONCRETE

FIRE
BRICK

SECTION "C-C"
FIG 3

TOP REENFORCING
1"x1" Ls WELDED

½ PLAN
"A-A"

C ─── C

G. I. PARTITION
IN CHIMNEY

FIRE BRICK

FIRE
BRICK

STONE
MASONRY

11" ±   14" ±   11" ±

½ PLAN "B-B"
FIG 4

C.I. FUEL GRATE

ASH
PIT

GROUND LINE

CONCRETE

VARIATION SECT.
[ASH PIT ADDED]
FIG 5

12" 6" 0   1'-0"   2'-0"   3'-0"   4'-0"   5'-0"   6'-0"   7'-0"

SCALE

PLATE XIII

PATENTED STOVE TYPE

THERE are a number of types of patented stoves adapted for use on camp grounds and picnic areas. These stoves are apparently designed primarily for cooking purposes, and the author has seen few of these patented stoves which, either before or after being covered with a stone masonry "shell", seem appropriate in a forest setting. They are excellently adapted to the more intensively used camp ground and picnic areas, near the centers of considerable population. The shape and appearance of these units are such that they do not seem to blend happily with the natural surroundings.

DESIGN AND CONSTRUCTION

Many of the patented stoves do not have a chimney. They are designed with an opening at the back of the irebox. The draft control, fire box, hearth, top grate or plate, and other mechanical features vary with each type of patented stove, and the stone masonry work should conform to the particular type of construction.

Unless the patented stove has a metal back and sides, a fire-clay brick lining should form a part of the enclosing masonry shell.

It is customary to provide, in the construction of these stoves, a ventilating air-space (see fig. 4), between the metal and the masonry. This air-space ought to be thoroughly sealed at the top.

The sketch in figure 2 shows another type of stove enclosed in a stone masonry covering. The use of this type of stove with the square metal chimney as shown in the sketch, gives rise to considerable difference of opinion concerning the appropriateness of this kind of a chimney to the forest surroundings.

There may be a few instances in which it is more desirable to use an inconspicuous, although distinctly artificial chimney of this type than to construct a massive chimney which is equally as far out of proportion to the camp stove. In general, the use of this type of stove, with the chimney as shown in the sketch, ought to be discouraged in spite of its practical value.

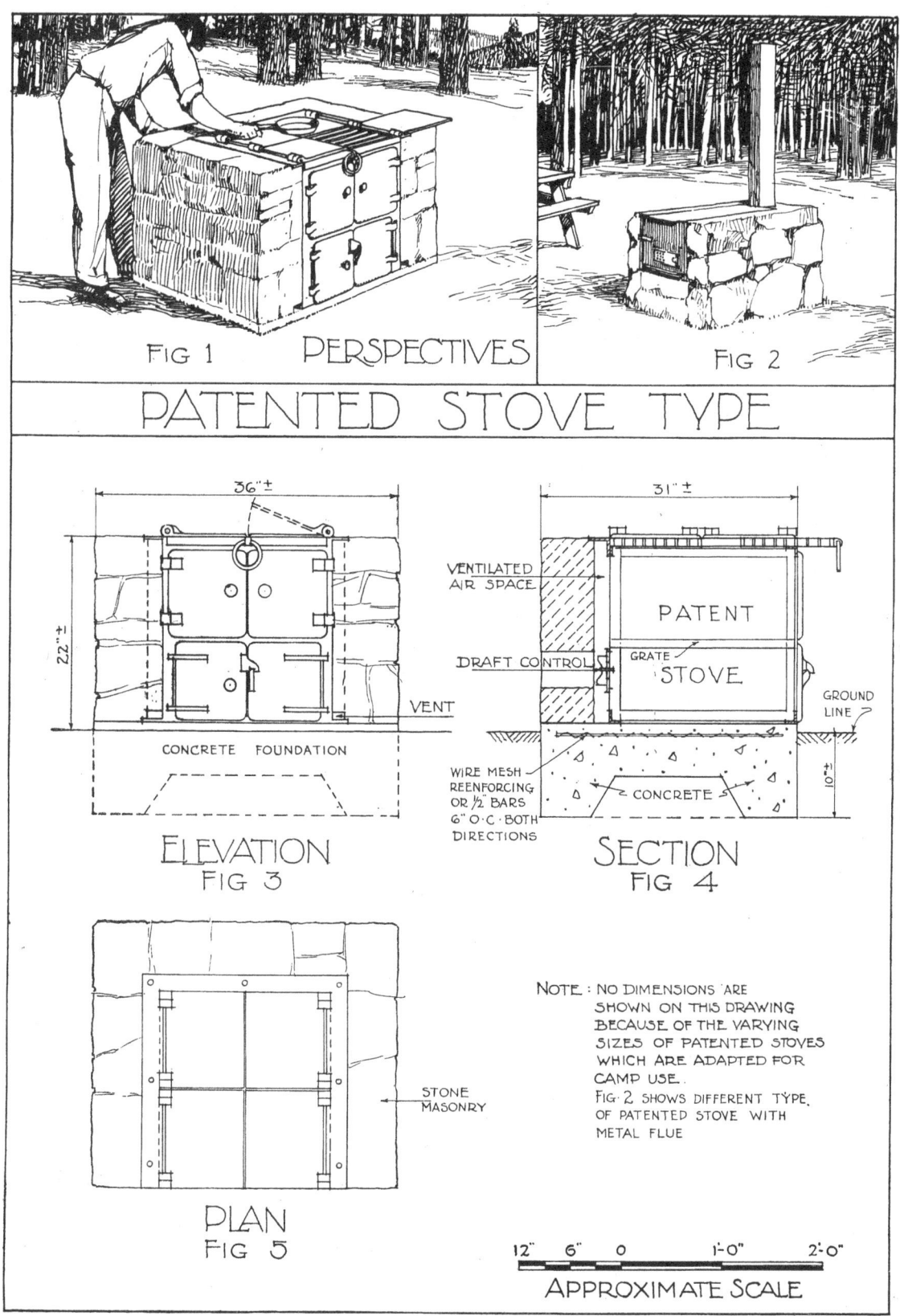

FIG 1   PERSPECTIVES   FIG 2

PATENTED STOVE TYPE

36"±

22"±

CONCRETE FOUNDATION

VENT

ELEVATION
FIG 3

31"±

VENTILATED
AIR SPACE

DRAFT CONTROL

PATENT

GRATE

STOVE

GROUND
LINE

WIRE MESH
REENFORCING
OR ½" BARS
6" O·C· BOTH
DIRECTIONS

CONCRETE

1'-0"±

SECTION
FIG 4

STONE
MASONRY

PLAN
FIG 5

NOTE : NO DIMENSIONS ARE
SHOWN ON THIS DRAWING
BECAUSE OF THE VARYING
SIZES OF PATENTED STOVES
WHICH ARE ADAPTED FOR
CAMP USE.
FIG 2 SHOWS DIFFERENT TYPE
OF PATENTED STOVE WITH
METAL FLUE

12"   6"   0   1'-0"   2'-0"

APPROXIMATE SCALE

PLATE XIV

WARMING-COOKING UNIT

ADAPTATION TO LOCATION AND USE

The warming-cooking unit is generally not adapted to areas where the fire hazard is great.

These units may be used, (a) in connection with shelters (pl. XIX, figs. 1 and 5), (b) in connection with swimming pools on campground areas, and (c) on campground and picnic areas. The two most logical ways in which to combine the campfire and the fireplace, or camp stove, are shown in figures 4 and 5 on the accompanying plate.

When these units are used in connection with shelters, it is the usual practice to face the camp fire toward the shelter, as shown on plate XIX, figure 6, and to have the cooking unit on the side farthest from the shelter. In this way the interior of the shelter receives the full benefit from the campfire, the purpose of which may be to warm and to light the interior of the shelter.

The warming fire by itself is another feature which is considered in connection with the discussion of plate XX.

These units are adapted only to areas where there is an adequate supply of fuel easily available.

DESIGN AND CONSTRUCTION

The design of the stonework should be very informal and rustic. The foundation under these features should extend below frost. It may be advisable to line the sides of the warming fire area with fire-clay brick or lava rock in order to protect the stone masonry from damage by the intense heat. The fire-clay brick lining should, however, be avoided if possible, even to the height of a few courses, because it is unsightly and unnatural in a fireplace of this type.

The top of the grate or the plate may be lowered to a height of 14 to 16 inches above the ground.

VARIATIONS IN DESIGN

The variations in design are shown in figures 4 and 5.

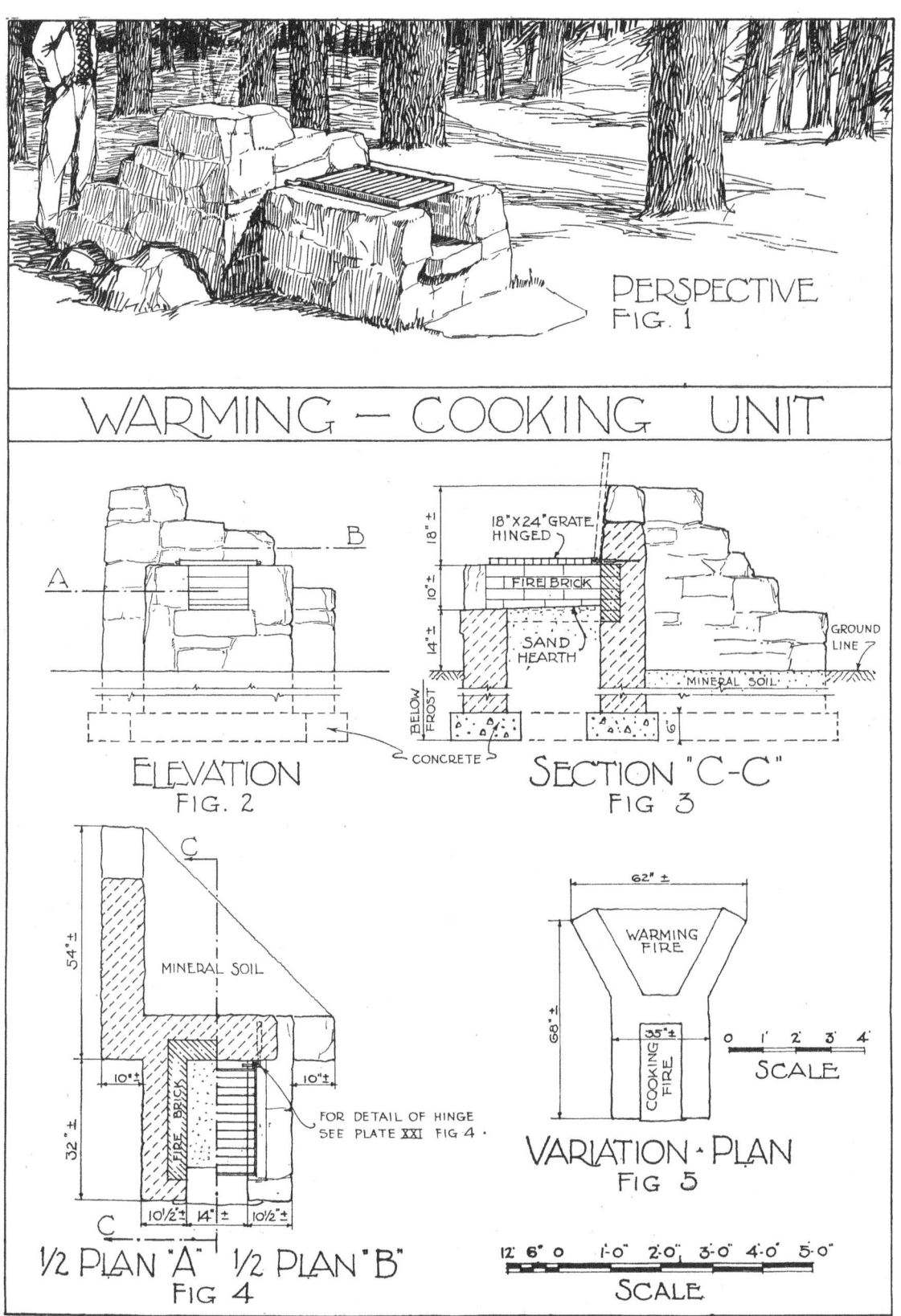

PERSPECTIVE
FIG. 1

WARMING — COOKING UNIT

ELEVATION
FIG. 2

18" X 24" GRATE HINGED
FIRE BRICK
SAND HEARTH
GROUND LINE
MINERAL SOIL
BELOW FROST
CONCRETE

SECTION "C-C"
FIG 3

54" ±
MINERAL SOIL
10" ±
32" ±
FIRE BRICK
10½" ± 14" ± 10½" ±
FOR DETAIL OF HINGE
SEE PLATE XXI FIG 4.

½ PLAN "A" ½ PLAN "B"
FIG 4

62" ±
WARMING FIRE
68" ±
35" ±
COOKING FIRE

VARIATION · PLAN
FIG 5

SCALE
0 1' 2' 3' 4'

SCALE
12' 6" 0 1'-0" 2'-0" 3'-0" 4'-0" 5'-0"

PLATE XV

BARBECUE PITS AND BARBECUE OVENS

GENERAL CONSIDERATIONS

While barbecue pits and barbecue ovens have been in use during a considerable period of years, the specific information relating particularly to the design and construction of these features is rather difficult to procure. The three types, as follow: (a) Barbecue pit (pl. XVI), (b) free standing barbecue oven (pl. XVII), and (c) hillside barbecue oven (pl. XVIII), shown in the accompanying plates, include the range of facilities normally used for barbecuing.

The word "barbecue" (both as a noun and a verb) is used in connection with the roasting of the whole carcass of an animal, or, for convenience in handling, the carcass is sometimes quartered or cut into even smaller portions.

For the purposes of this bulletin, only the medium-sized barbecue pit and oven is shown in the detailed drawings. The larger barbecue pits and ovens, when required, are designed in accordance with the same plans, and the size is computed in accordance with the requirements of use, as hereafter explained.

LOCATIONS FOR BARBECUE PITS AND BARBECUE OVENS

These features are of practical use only where large numbers of people congregate in the open to eat at the same time. The specific location selected for barbecue pits, in particular, must be well drained, because any fire built in the bottom of a pit would not operate efficiently if free moisture were present to choke out the fire. The presence of an abnormal amount of moisture would cause the formation of steam, and might even cause an explosion.

There should be a reasonably large open and flat area adjacent to the barbecue pit or oven, in order that all of the people who are likely to gather for any such occasion may be accommodated.

The construction of barbecue features is expensive, and the successful operation of the barbecue pit or barbecue oven consumes a large quantity of wood. These features should therefore be constructed only where the supply of natural fuel is plentiful, and where there is a real demand for the use of this kind of a cooking facility.

In Puerto Rico, where the climate permits outdoor activity during the entire year, and where roast pig is considered a real delicacy, barbecue pits and ovens are almost a necessity in connection with public recreation areas.

ADAPTATION TO USE

Barbecue facilities are adapted to the roasting of an entire carcass or to one or more large portions of meat at the same time.

The successful operation of a barbecue pit or oven requires an experienced individual who understands this method of cooking meat. Inexperienced operators may easily spoil meat by under- or over-cooking it through incorrect operation of the barbecue pit or oven.

The real purpose of the barbecue pit and barbecue oven is that of slowly cooking a considerable quantity of meat for a period of time which may vary from 8 to 12 hours, and sometimes 24 to 36 hours, depending upon the size of the carcass and the degree of heat.

The maximum success in barbecuing meat is procured when the pit or oven can be made practically airtight and thus resembling a fireless cooker. Unless the pit is practically airtight, the meat is very apt to burn.

OPERATION OF BARBECUE PIT AND OVEN

While barbecue pits and ovens possess the advantage of providing facilities for the cooking of a considerable quantity of meat at one time, these features also have the disadvantage of being difficult to operate conveniently, because of the intense heat and the unwieldiness of the ordinary-sized carcass of a steer or other animal, unless the barbecue feature is well designed for practical operation. The practical methods of handling large pieces of meat are explained in the text which accompanies the following plates.

DETERMINING SIZE OF BARBECUE PIT OR OVEN

The actual size of the barbecue pit or barbecue oven is determined by the number of people for whom a supply of meat must be barbecued at any one time. In determining the practical size for any specific area, it is necessary first to determine the number of people who will occupy, at any one time, a recreation area provided with barbecue facilities.

It is generally estimated that 1 cubic foot of meat weighs approximately 40 pounds, and that the allowance per person will vary from one-half to 1 pound, depending upon the extent to which other foods are supplied for any specific occasion. The estimated amount of meat consumed per person will also depend upon the percentage of bone which remains in any carcass to be barbecued (allowance of 20 percent is usually made for the bone, unless the section of beef has been boned) and it will also depend upon the amount of waste due to undesirable cuts and excessive fat. The skill and ingenuity of the operator in properly cooking and properly cutting the meat when served also is a factor.

It is further generally assumed that there ought to be approximately 12 inches of clearance between all confining surfaces and the meat. A cubic foot of meat would therefore properly fit into a barbecue pit or barbecue oven with dimensions 3 feet wide, 3 feet long, and 3 feet high, making allowance for the depth of ashes which would remain in the bottom of the barbecue pit, but no allowance for any ashes in the bottom of the barbecue oven (inasmuch as the ashes would be removed from the bottom of the oven before the meat is put in place). This size of meat would therefore serve from 40 to 80 persons, depending upon the conditions above stated.

On the basis of this analysis, the number of people who could be served at any one time through the cooking facilities of the barbecue pits and ovens in the following drawings would be approximately as follows:

Barbecue pit shown in plate XVI (with capacity of approximately 310 pounds)—number of people to be served approximates from 350 to 600.

Plate XVII—number of people to be served approximates from 250 to 475.

Plate XVIII—number of people to be served approximates from 450 to 875.

MATERIALS OF CONSTRUCTION

The materials of construction are covered in the detailed discussion which accompanies each of the following plates.

In general, it is desirable that the barbecue pit and barbecue oven should be properly lined with fire-clay brick, although a lining of dense volcanic rock would also serve in place of the fire-clay brick.

METHOD OF OPERATION

In the successful operation of a barbecue pit or barbecue oven, the meat is cooked by the heat which is retained in the surrounding walls and floor of the barbecue pit or oven.

There are several ways of preparing meat for barbecuing. The most common way is to take the cleaned and skinned carcass and roast it whole, without removing any bones.

Oftentimes, larger animals are quartered, or cut into even smaller portions, each weighing from 40 to 50 pounds, to facilitate the ease of handling. When the meat is thus cut, the individual pieces should be of approximately equal size, in order that each piece may cook uniformly. The usual procedure is to tie the pieces of meat with heavy twine, like rolled roasts of beef.

Sometimes a method of barbecuing called steam roasting is adopted, in which case the pieces of meat are wrapped in wax paper and covered by damp clean sacks before being placed in the pit or oven. This method of procedure preserves the juices in the meat and gives a less-pronounced roasted taste.

It is necessary, in cooking the meat, that the cover to the pit, or the doors to the oven, should be replaced and the cooking space sealed as tightly as possible immediately after putting the meat in place.

An exclusion of air from the pit and the oven during the cooking process is very important, in order to insure that the meat will be brown in color, tender, and not burned, and also in order that the meat shall retain its natural flavor.

BARBECUE PIT

THE barbecue pit offers the simplest means of maintaining the necessary degree of heat for barbecuing. The Indians and the early settlers discovered long ago that a hastily dug hole or trench, in the bottom of which were placed large stones, and on the top of which had been built a hot fire, was an excellent means of cooking large portions of meat.

Wherever the ground is sufficiently well drained to make practical the construction of a pit, the barbecue pit is preferable to the barbecue oven, because the natural ground serves to insulate the area surrounding the pit and preserves the maximum amount of heat.

The walls of the pit may be made of concrete or stone masonry and the sides of the pit lined with fire-clay brick, as shown in plate XVI. The floor of the pit should be of pervious soil to provide ready drainage and, if desirable, to imbed in this soil a few larger stones, in order to retain some of the heat in the bottom of the pit.

A fire may readily be made in the pit by inserting one or two posts in an upright position, and heaping the wood around these posts. After the wood has been put in place, the posts are then withdrawn and a small amount of kerosene or other oil may be poured into the hole, and the wood ignited by a burning torch dropped into the hole.

This fire thus started in the pit (depending upon the size of the pit) should be kept burning for a period of 8 or 12 hours or longer, in order to thoroughly heat the bottom and side walls, and to create a bed of ashes over the bottom of the pit.

After the fire thus maintained has thoroughly heated the pit, the carcass or chunks of meat are put into place in a wire basket, as shown in figures 1 and 5 of the accompanying plate. The cover to the pit may consist of a pair of hinged boiler-plate doors, reinforced with 2- by 3-inch angles to prevent any sagging of the doors.

As shown in the drawing, these doors have large handles through which a pole may be inserted to facilitate lifting. Free standing posts support the doors when the pit is open and prevent straining of the hinges.

The basket is made of woven wire and is suspended from two pipes, which rest in grooves at the ends of the wall, as shown in figures 2 and 3.

After the meat is put in place, the covers to the pit are closed and earth is banked over the top of the covers to prevent any unnecessary loss of heat and to increase the airtight condition of the pit.

When the pit is not in operation, provisions should be made so that the covers may be locked, in order to prevent vandalism and to avoid accidents.

In many places in the western part of the country, food is cooked in a "dutch" oven, which is a small unit (pl. XI–A), operating on the principle of the barbeque pit. The container, which resembles a large kettle, is made of cast iron and has a tight fitting cover. A fire is built, and a liberal bed of live coals is produced by burning the fire for the desired length of time to produce enough coals so that this "dutch" oven may be partly buried in the coals and the remainder of the coals may then be heaped against the sides and over the top of this container in which the food is placed. This method of cooking requires considerable skill to know the length of time which will be required in order to properly cook different kinds of meat and other food. The "dutch" oven, so-called, can usually be purchased from hardware stores in the western part of the country, and it is in general use by the sheep-herders and others who wish to have an efficient and compact unit in which to cook food.

BARBECUE PIT

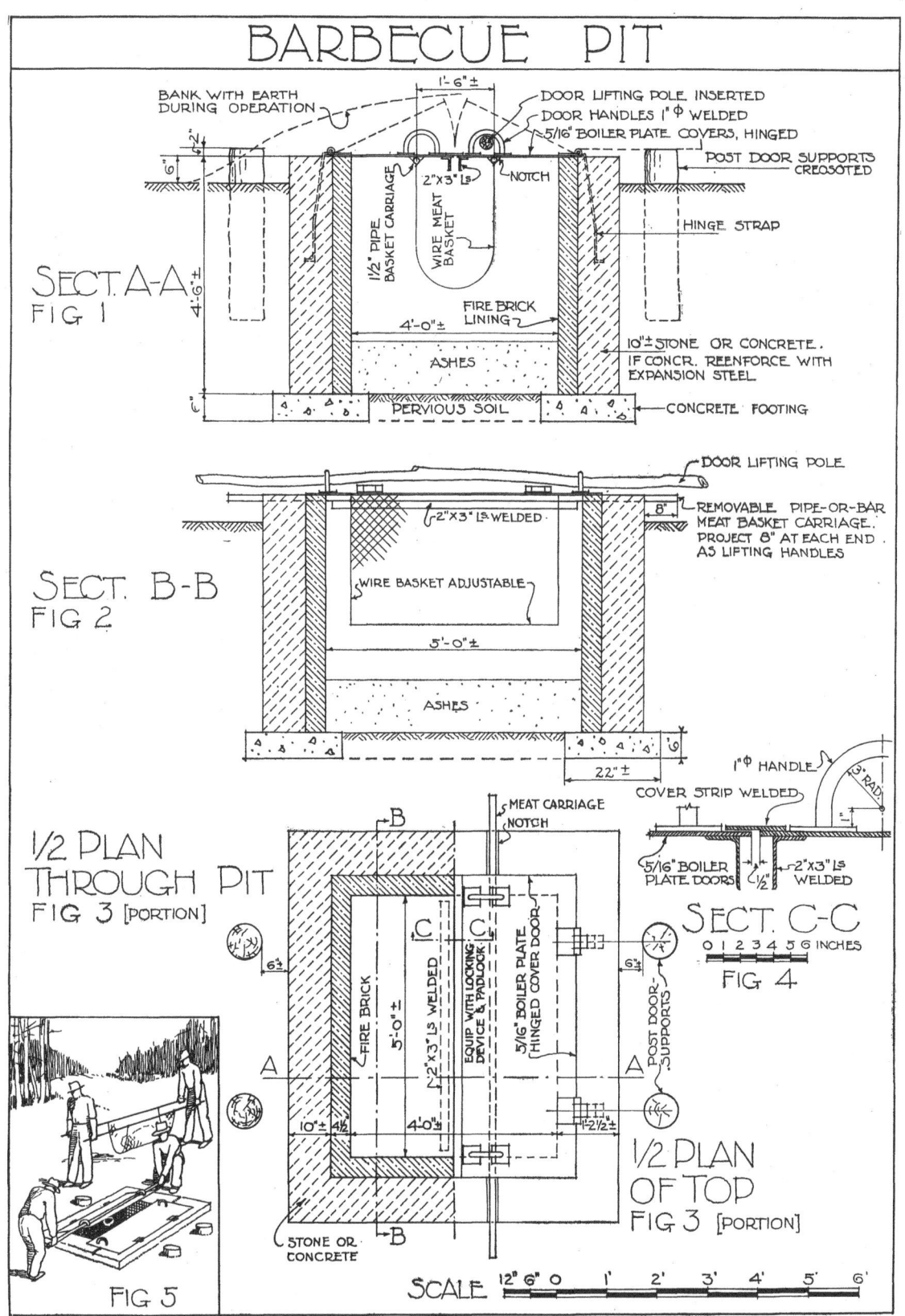

SECT. A-A
FIG 1

BANK WITH EARTH DURING OPERATION

DOOR LIFTING POLE INSERTED
DOOR HANDLES 1"⌀ WELDED
5/16" BOILER PLATE COVERS, HINGED
POST DOOR SUPPORTS CREOSOTED
NOTCH
1'-6"±
2"x3" Ls
1½" PIPE BASKET CARRIAGE
WIRE MEAT BASKET
HINGE STRAP
2"
6"
4'-6"±
FIRE BRICK LINING
4'-0"±
ASHES
10"± STONE OR CONCRETE. IF CONCR. REENFORCE WITH EXPANSION STEEL
6"
PERVIOUS SOIL
CONCRETE FOOTING

SECT. B-B
FIG 2

DOOR LIFTING POLE
2"x3" Ls WELDED
WIRE BASKET ADJUSTABLE
5'-0"±
ASHES
8"
REMOVABLE PIPE-OR-BAR MEAT BASKET CARRIAGE. PROJECT 8" AT EACH END AS LIFTING HANDLES
6"
22"±

½ PLAN THROUGH PIT
FIG 3 [PORTION]

B
MEAT CARRIAGE
NOTCH
C
C
6½
FIRE BRICK
5'-0"±
2"x3" Ls WELDED
EQUIP WITH LOCKING DEVICE & PADLOCK
5/16" BOILER PLATE HINGED COVER DOOR
A
A
POST DOOR SUPPORTS
10"± 4½
4'-0"±
1-2½"
STONE OR CONCRETE
B

1"⌀ HANDLE
3" RAD.
COVER STRIP WELDED
5/16" BOILER PLATE DOORS
½
2"x3" Ls WELDED
1"
SECT. C-C
0 1 2 3 4 5 6 INCHES
FIG 4

6½

½ PLAN OF TOP
FIG 3 [PORTION]

FIG 5

SCALE   12" 6" 0   1'   2'   3'   4'   5'   6'

PLATE XVI

63

BARBECUE OVEN

IN SOME locations, where the natural drainage facilities are not acceptable for barbecue pits, it is advisable to construct barbecue ovens.

The most desirable type of barbecue oven is the type such as is shown in plate XVIII, which is constructed in a slope so that the front of the oven is the only evident part of the artificial construction.

It is necessary, however, in some locations, on the flat areas, to construct a barbecue oven entirely above ground, as shown in plate XVII. The question of proper insulation for conserving the maximum amount of heat within the oven, is a primary consideration. One method of construction, in order to accomplish this result, is shown in the detailed drawings in plate XVII, through which method of construction an air space is provided between the fire-clay brick lining and the outer stone masonry shell.

In these ovens, not only the side walls and the roof, but also the floor, is of fire-clay brick. This fire-clay brick floor is laid upon a reenforced concrete base. After the oven has been thoroughly heated, the ashes are raked from the oven before the meat is placed in the oven on the grill which is shown in the detailed drawing.

In this type of feature, the stone-masonry walls must be carried below the frost-line.

The constructing of this type of barbecue oven requires that the fire-clay brick shell shall first be constructed on the concrete foundation. The centering is then put in place, and the outer stone masonry shell is constructed.

The wood members used for the centering are thoroughly soaked before being put in place, so that there can be no subsequent swelling which might injure the structure.

It does not matter what happens to this centering after the construction has been completed. In all probability it will shrink and drop out of place, and it will probably char, without affecting in any perceptible degree, the insulating qualities.

In all barbecue ovens, a chimney is necessary. This chimney will have a flue lining, which should be supported on iron straps, as shown in figure 2. These straps are supports for a removable plate, which is put in place after the fire has been removed. In order to properly seal this part of the oven, natural earth is placed on the top of the plate in the flue, as shown in figure 5.

The grill, of reenforcing mesh (fig. 3), on which the meat is placed is supported by ¾-inch rods, as shown in figures 2 and 5.

After the meat has been placed in the oven, the front opening is closed with a double covering consisting of an inner shield of sheet-iron (fig. 5), which is locked in place during the actual cooking operation. A small amount of natural earth, placed at the bottom of the inner shield, may help to seal this opening.

The doors are then closed and locked, and it might be advisable to place a small amount of earth against the bottom of the doors.

When not in use, the main outside doors should be kept fastened with a padlock.

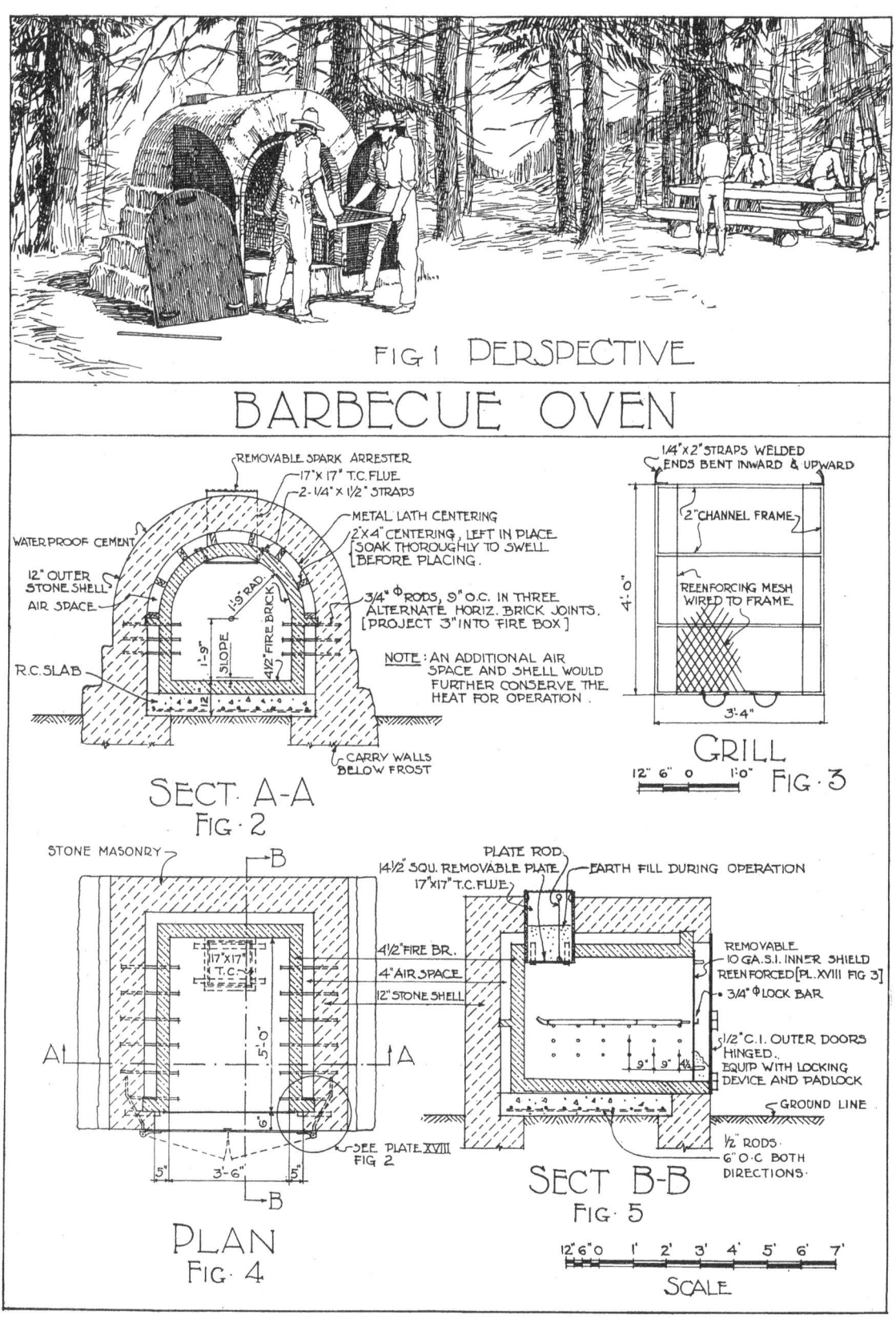

FIG 1 PERSPECTIVE

BARBECUE OVEN

SECT A-A
FIG·2

- REMOVABLE SPARK ARRESTER
- 17"X 17" T.C. FLUE
- 2-1/4"X 1/2" STRAPS
- METAL LATH CENTERING
- 2"X4" CENTERING, LEFT IN PLACE. SOAK THOROUGHLY TO SWELL BEFORE PLACING.
- 3/4"⌀ RODS, 9" O.C. IN THREE ALTERNATE HORIZ. BRICK JOINTS. [PROJECT 3" INTO FIRE BOX]

WATER PROOF CEMENT

12" OUTER STONE SHELL
AIR SPACE

R.C. SLAB

1'-9" RAD.
SLOPE
1'-9"
4 1/2" FIRE BRICK

<u>NOTE</u>: AN ADDITIONAL AIR SPACE AND SHELL WOULD FURTHER CONSERVE THE HEAT FOR OPERATION.

CARRY WALLS BELOW FROST

GRILL FIG·3

- 1/4"X 2" STRAPS WELDED ENDS BENT INWARD & UPWARD
- 2" CHANNEL FRAME
- REENFORCING MESH WIRED TO FRAME

4'-0"
3'-4"

12" 6" 0   1'-0"

PLAN
FIG·4

STONE MASONRY

17"X17" T.C.

5'-0"

A

B

6"
5'   3'-6"   5'

SEE PLATE XVIII FIG 2

4 1/2" FIRE BR.
4" AIR SPACE
12" STONE SHELL

SECT B-B
FIG·5

- PLATE ROD
- 14 1/2" SQU. REMOVABLE PLATE
- 17"X17" T.C. FLUE
- EARTH FILL DURING OPERATION
- REMOVABLE 10 GA. S.I. INNER SHIELD REENFORCED [PL. XVIII FIG 3]
- 3/4"⌀ LOCK BAR
- 1/2" C.I. OUTER DOORS HINGED. EQUIP WITH LOCKING DEVICE AND PADLOCK
- GROUND LINE
- 1/2" RODS 6" O.C BOTH DIRECTIONS

9" 9" 4 1/2"

12" 6" 0   1'   2'   3'   4'   5'   6'   7'

SCALE

PLATE XVII

HILLSIDE BARBECUE OVEN

THE hillside barbecue oven, where natural conditions of topography are adapted to the construction of this type of oven, is preferable to the free standing oven shown in plate XVII because this unit is not as conspicuous.

Construction of the hillside barbecue oven is substantially the same as of the free standing oven, except that the natural earth covering makes it unnecessary to provide the insulating air space between the back of the fire-clay brick lining and the inside surface of the stone masonry shell.

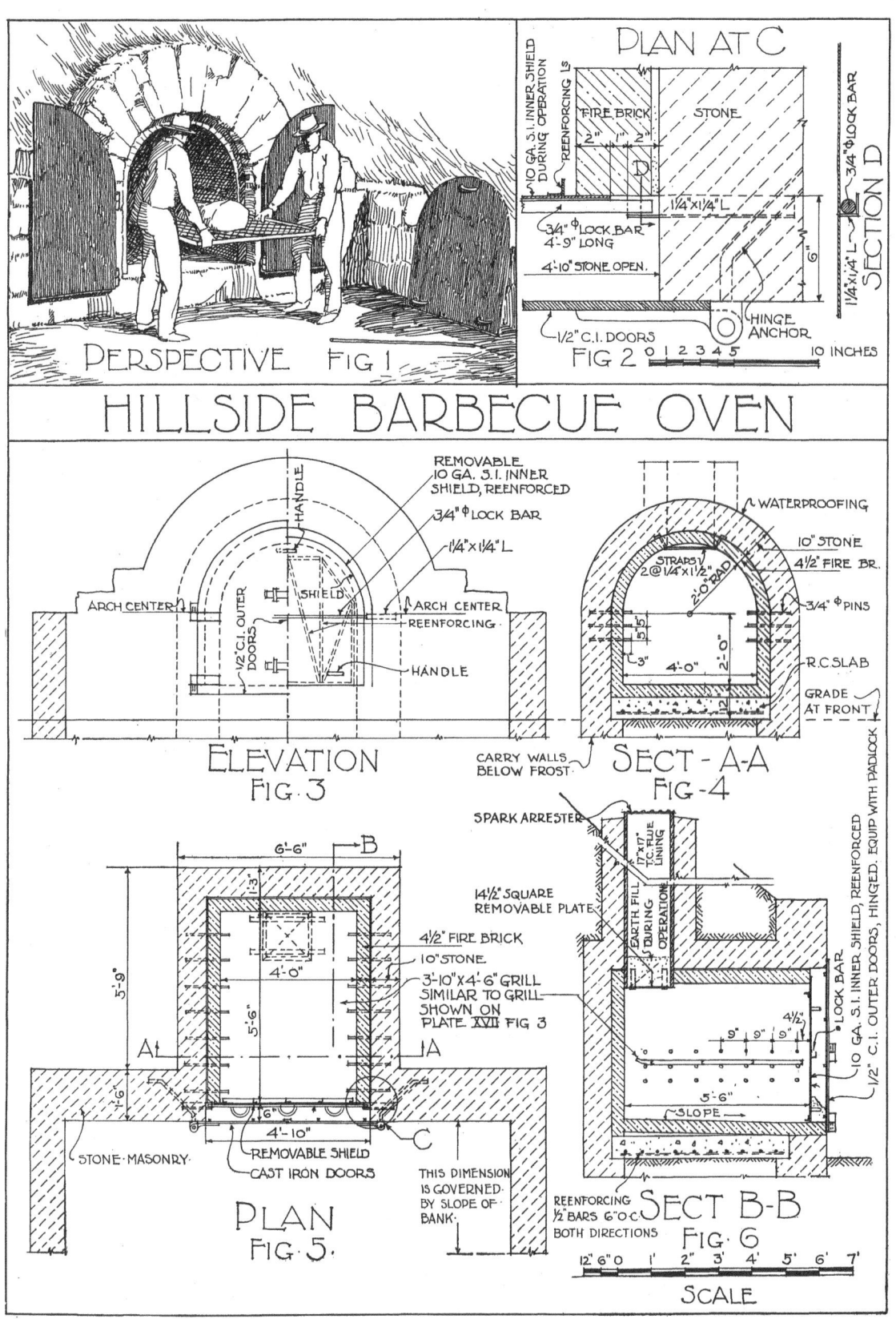

PLAN AT C

REENFORCING 1s
10 GA. S.I. INNER SHIELD
DURING OPERATION
FIRE BRICK   STONE
2" 1" 2"
D
3/4"Φ LOCK BAR
1/4"x1/4" L
3/4" Φ LOCK BAR
4'-9" LONG
1/4"x1/4" L
4'-10" STONE OPEN.
SECTION D
6"
1/2" C.I. DOORS
HINGE ANCHOR
FIG 2   0 1 2 3 4 5   10 INCHES

PERSPECTIVE   FIG 1

HILLSIDE BARBECUE OVEN

REMOVABLE
10 GA. S.I. INNER
SHIELD, REENFORCED
3/4"Φ LOCK BAR
1/4"x1/4" L
HANDLE
SHIELD
ARCH CENTER
ARCH CENTER
REENFORCING
1/2" C.I. OUTER
DOORS
HANDLE

ELEVATION
FIG 3

WATERPROOFING
10" STONE
4 1/2" FIRE BR.
STRAPS
2 @ 1/4"x1 1/2"
2'-0" RAD
3/4" Φ PINS
5'-5"
3"
4'-0"   2'-0"
R.C. SLAB
GRADE
AT FRONT

CARRY WALLS
BELOW FROST

SECT - A-A
FIG - 4

6'-6"   B
1'-3"
5'-9"
5'-6"
4'-0"
A   A
1'-6"
6"
4'-10"
STONE MASONRY
REMOVABLE SHIELD
CAST IRON DOORS
C
THIS DIMENSION
IS GOVERNED
BY SLOPE OF
BANK.

4 1/2" FIRE BRICK
10" STONE
3'-10"x4'-6" GRILL
SIMILAR TO GRILL
SHOWN ON
PLATE XVII FIG 3

PLAN
FIG 5.

SPARK ARRESTER
14 1/2" SQUARE
REMOVABLE PLATE
17"x17"
T.C. FLUE
LINING
EARTH FILL
DURING
OPERATION
LOCK BAR
10 GA. S.I. INNER SHIELD, REENFORCED
1/2" C.I. OUTER DOORS, HINGED. EQUIP WITH PADLOCK
9" 9" 9"   4 1/2"
5'-6"
SLOPE
REENFORCING
1/2" BARS 6'0"C.
BOTH DIRECTIONS

SECT B-B
FIG · 6

12" 6" 0   1'   2'   3'   4'   5'   6'   7'
SCALE

PLATE XVIII

FIREPLACE SHELTER TYPES

THE fireplace shelter has proved to be a very desirable feature on many campgrounds and along numerous trails. In some parts of the country where there is considerable possibility of heavy storms during the recreation season these shelters are essential. The shelters along the trails are usually located in the more remote portions of the forest to accommodate hikers and horseback riders who use these trails during the early spring and the late fall. Properly located shelters along these trails also provide effective protection in case of sudden storms by affording a place in which to get away from rain and cold. Shelters of the character such as are indicated in plate XIX, if appropriately designed to be adapted to the use imposed upon them, are most desirable.

These shelters are of three kinds:

(a) Shelter with a fireplace or combination stove and fireplace constructed in front of the shelter (figs. 1 and 5).
(b) Shelters with the fireplace or combination stove and fireplace constructed within the shelter (fig. 3).
(c) Shelters with a fireplace within the shelter and a camp stove in front of the shelter.

The problem of locating the camp stove in relation to the front of the shelter is important. The shelter must be so oriented that the prevailing winds will not carry the smoke from the fireplace into the shelter. To be practical the distance between the front line of the shelter and the front of the fireplace should not be greater than 8 feet. If the fireplace is closer to the shelter, the heat may be uncomfortable unless the shelter is abnormally deep. If the fireplace is too far removed from the shelter, then it serves no practical purpose for providing heat within the shelter during the cold rainy days and during the early morning and evening hours in the spring and fall.

When the shelter is located along the trails and roads, especially in the mountains, these structures should be so located that the front of the shelter will command important views of the fine mountain scenery.

The design for the shelter may be that of a single sloping roof (fig. 5) or with a gable end (fig. 1). Shelters are constructed of boards or preferably of logs, and in a few instances they may be of stone masonry construction.

The size of the shelter should be such that there is ample space under the roof to provide for one single bed on either side of the shelter, a small table and the necessary seating accommodations. The approximate dimensions of the average shelter are 10 to 12 feet in width and from 12 to 15 feet in depth.

Where a fireplace is constructed in the rear wall of the shelter, it is desirable that the shelter be somewhat larger than the above measurements. A fireplace so located is a very useful feature especially in parts of the country where frequent rains cause considerable inconvenience in cooking out of doors.

The fireplace usually constructed at the front of the shelter may serve two purposes: (a) As a warming fire and (b) as a cooking fire. A combination warming and cooking unit, similar to that shown in plate XV is probably the most practical unit to be used in connection with shelter. Where the fireplace type is used, those types which are best adapted for this use are shown in plates VI, VIII, IX, X, and XI.

The fundamental principles of design to be followed in developing the fireplace within the shelter are shown in plate XXIII.

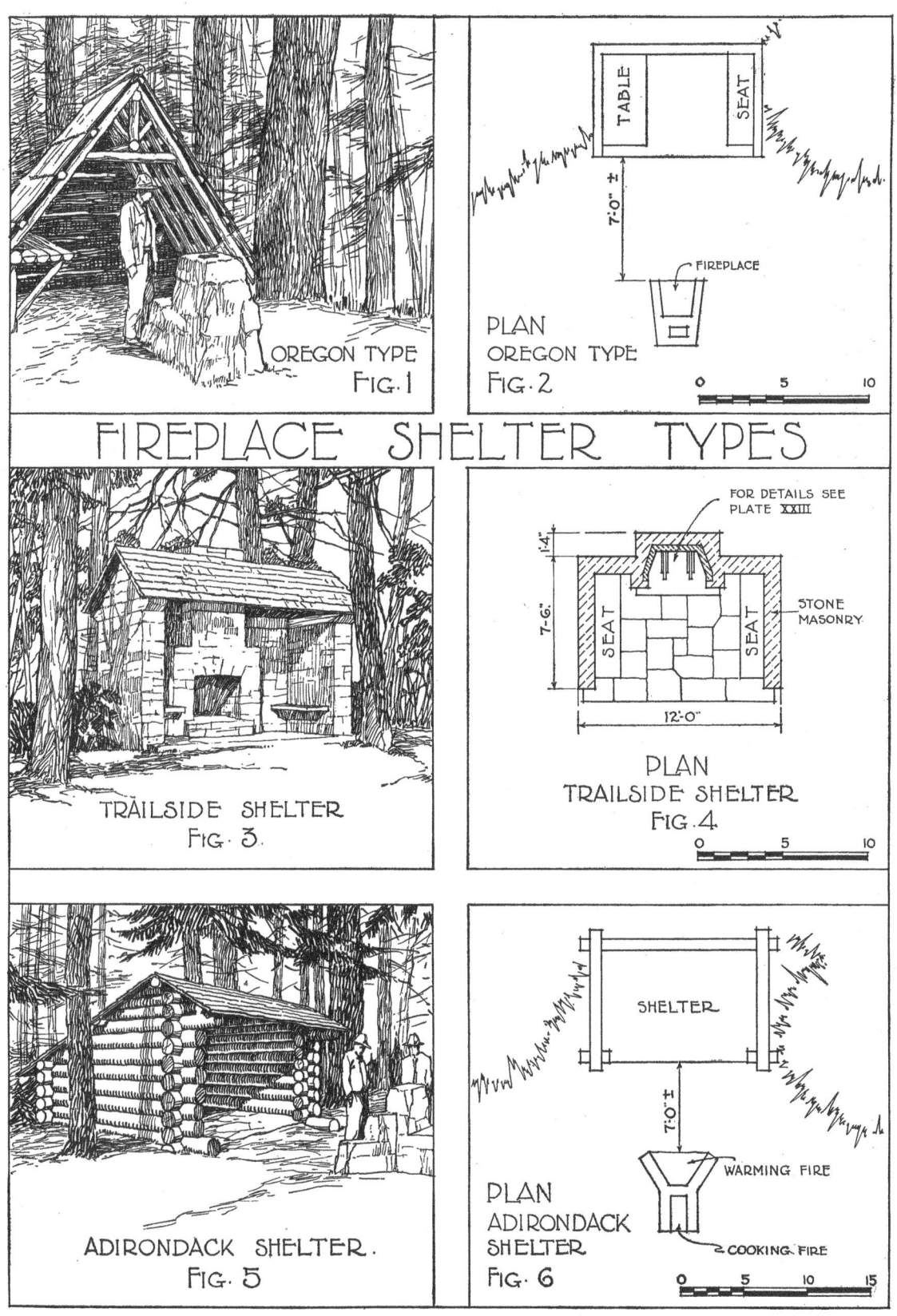

FIREPLACE SHELTER TYPES

OREGON TYPE
FIG. 1

PLAN
OREGON TYPE
FIG. 2

TABLE

SEAT

7'-0" ±

FIREPLACE

0   5   10

TRAILSIDE SHELTER
FIG. 3.

PLAN
TRAILSIDE SHELTER
FIG. 4

FOR DETAILS SEE
PLATE XXIII

1'-4"

7'-6"

SEAT

SEAT

STONE
MASONRY

12'-0"

0   5   10

ADIRONDACK SHELTER.
FIG. 5

PLAN
ADIRONDACK
SHELTER
FIG. 6

SHELTER

7'-0" ±

WARMING FIRE

COOKING FIRE

0   5   10   15

PLATE XIX

WARMING FIRES AND CAMP FIRES

THE Mount Hood type of warming fire (fig. 1) is used in connection with swimming pools on forest campgrounds, and it provides a feature around which the bathers may sit to dry themselves after a plunge in cool waters. The temperature of the air among the large timber of some of the mountain forests is cool even during the many warm days of the summer months and these warming fires are a welcome feature. The splayed sides (fig. 2) provide a surface which reflects a maximum amount of heat.

There are three kinds of open fires: (a) The bonfire; (b) the campfire; (c) the open fireplace.

This part of the discussion is confined to the campfire, which may be for community-camp use or for individual groups of campers. The bonfire is a feature similar to the campfire, but larger, and usually for large groups.

The campfire is generally developed within a circular area which is well defined by a border of stones (preferably small boulders). This campfire may be for community groups or for single camp groups.

In the center of the campfire circle it is oftentimes desirable to construct an upright post of concrete or of iron against which the logs may rest, thus developing a more attractive fire than can be produced by laying the logs in horizontal position.

The small campfire circle (fig. 5) may also be used for cooking purposes, as shown in the sketch and in the accompanying plan (fig. 6).

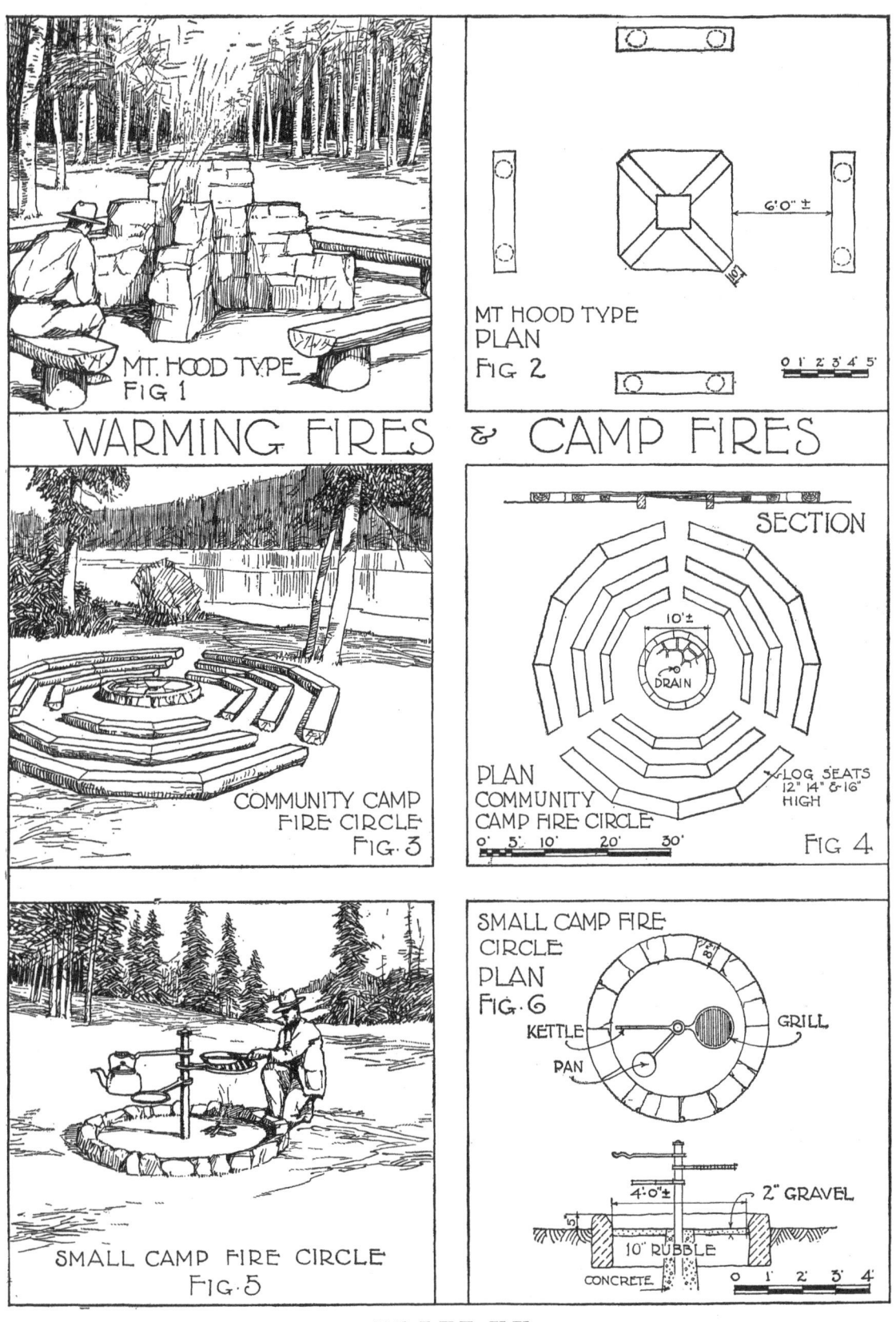

MT. HOOD TYPE
FIG 1

MT HOOD TYPE
PLAN
FIG 2

6'0" ±

0 1 2 3 4 5

WARMING FIRES & CAMP FIRES

COMMUNITY CAMP
FIRE CIRCLE
FIG. 3

SECTION

10' ±

DRAIN

PLAN
COMMUNITY
CAMP FIRE CIRCLE

LOG SEATS
12" 14" & 16"
HIGH

0' 5' 10' 20' 30'

FIG 4

SMALL CAMP FIRE
CIRCLE
PLAN
FIG. 6

KETTLE

GRILL

PAN

4'0" ±

2" GRAVEL

10" RUBBLE

CONCRETE

0 1 2 3 4

SMALL CAMP FIRE CIRCLE
FIG. 5

PLATE XX

71

CONSTRUCTION DETAILS

FOR the successful design and construction of camp stoves and fireplaces, it is most essential that the details of design and construction should be given the most thorough consideration. Inasmuch as these details may apply to a number of types of camp stoves or fireplaces, it has been deemed advisable to arrange these construction details for ready reference, upon the following sheets (pls. XXI, XXII, and XXII–A).

There are a number of variations in these details and it is only the purpose of these three drawings to provide detailed information concerning the fundamental information which is necessary for reference in connection with construction details for these features.

CONSTRUCTION DETAILS

FIGURE 1

Section through firebox lined with $4\frac{1}{2}$ inches of fire-clay brick at sides and $2\frac{1}{2}$ inches of fire-clay brick on hearth. The grate is chained.

FIGURE 2

Section through firebox, with $2\frac{1}{2}$ inches of fire-clay brick side lining and hearth. The grate is hinged. (For hinge detail, see fig. 3.)

FIGURE 3

Grate hinge detail. The grate frame is extended at hinge side as shown—the ends being welded together. The extended portions have a $\frac{5}{8}$-inch diameter hole for passage of hinge rod. The $\frac{1}{2}$-inch diameter hinge rod is held in $\frac{3}{4}$-inch pipe sleeves built into the masonry.

FIGURE 4

A further development of the grate hinge shown in figure 3. Here a solid plate is hinged on to the same hinge rod carrying the grate. The solid plate may be thrown back independently of the grate; or both plate and grate may be thrown open, converting the fireplace into a warming reflector. In this detail, the hinge bars are two separate bent sections, with flattened ends, built into the chimney (also see pl. X).

FIGURE 5

Detail of built-in grate bars. The bars are let into pipe sleeves, allowing for expansion. They may or may not be arranged in such a way that removal and replacement can be taken care of in case of damage.

In plan B, the bolts near either end of the rod are removed. The rod is slipped back into one sleeve pocket, freeing the other end for complete removal.

In plan C, one or both ends of the rod, together with its pipe sleeve fitting, pass completely through the side walls of the fireplace, with bolts as shown, for securing the rod in place.

FIGURE 6

Eye bolt chain anchor.

FIGURE 7

Pin chain anchor.

In addition to types shown, the end of the chain may be spiked to a post, or log deadman sunk into the ground.

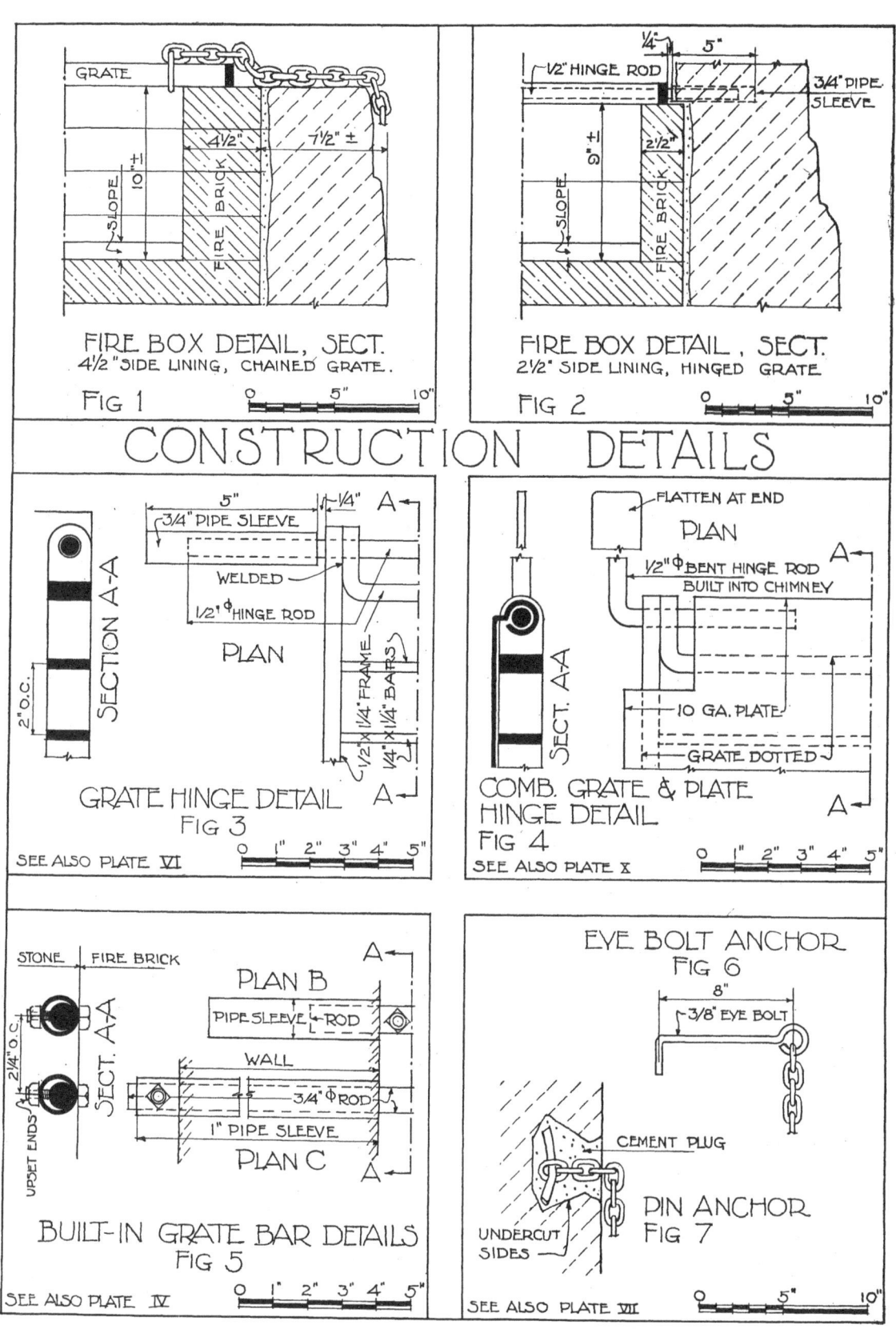

GRATE

4½" 7½" ±

10" ±

SLOPE

FIRE BRICK

FIRE BOX DETAIL, SECT.
4½" SIDE LINING, CHAINED GRATE.

FIG 1

0 5" 10"

½" HINGE ROD

¼" 5"

¾" PIPE SLEEVE

9" ±

2½"

SLOPE

FIRE BRICK

FIRE BOX DETAIL, SECT.
2½" SIDE LINING, HINGED GRATE

FIG 2

0 5" 10"

CONSTRUCTION DETAILS

SECTION A-A

2" O.C.

5" ¼" A

¾" PIPE SLEEVE

WELDED

½"φ HINGE ROD

PLAN

½" X ¼" FRAME

¼" X ¼" BARS

A

GRATE HINGE DETAIL
FIG 3

SEE ALSO PLATE VI

0 1" 2" 3" 4" 5"

FLATTEN AT END

PLAN

½"φ BENT HINGE ROD
BUILT INTO CHIMNEY

A

SECT. A-A

10 GA. PLATE

GRATE DOTTED

A

COMB. GRATE & PLATE
HINGE DETAIL
FIG 4

SEE ALSO PLATE X

0 1" 2" 3" 4" 5"

STONE FIRE BRICK

2¼" O.C.

UPSET ENDS

SECT. A-A

PLAN B

PIPE SLEEVE ROD

WALL

¾"φ ROD

1" PIPE SLEEVE

PLAN C

A

A

BUILT-IN GRATE BAR DETAILS
FIG 5

SEE ALSO PLATE IV

0 1" 2" 3" 4" 5"

EYE BOLT ANCHOR
FIG 6

8"

3/8" EYE BOLT

CEMENT PLUG

UNDERCUT
SIDES

PIN ANCHOR
FIG 7

SEE ALSO PLATE VII

0 5" 10"

PLATE XXI

CONSTRUCTION DETAILS

FIGURE 1

Wire-mesh grill details. A heavy woven mesh or reenforcing mesh is welded or hooked around a rod frame, and the resulting grate may either be chained to the fireplace or hinged, as shown, by means of eyebolt hinges.

FIGURE 2

There is great variance of opinion as to the respective merits of solid tops or open grates. Also as to the respective merits of cast iron and sheet iron. (See general discussion.) The various thicknesses are indicated.

FIGURE 3

A chimney is shown lined on the one hand with fire-clay brick, and, as a variation, with terra cotta flue lining.

"A", "B", and "C" show various types of spark arresters.

A damper is shown below.

FIGURE 4

Various designs of angle iron reenforcing are welded to the underside of the plates. Additional dispositions of the angles are possible in a number of ways. In the case of cast-iron tops, the reenforcing ribs are an integral part of the casting and by some persons the cast-iron top with such reenforcing is preferred.

Holes are conveniently spotted in the tops to facilitate easier handling.

Bent flanges may decrease the danger of sagging.

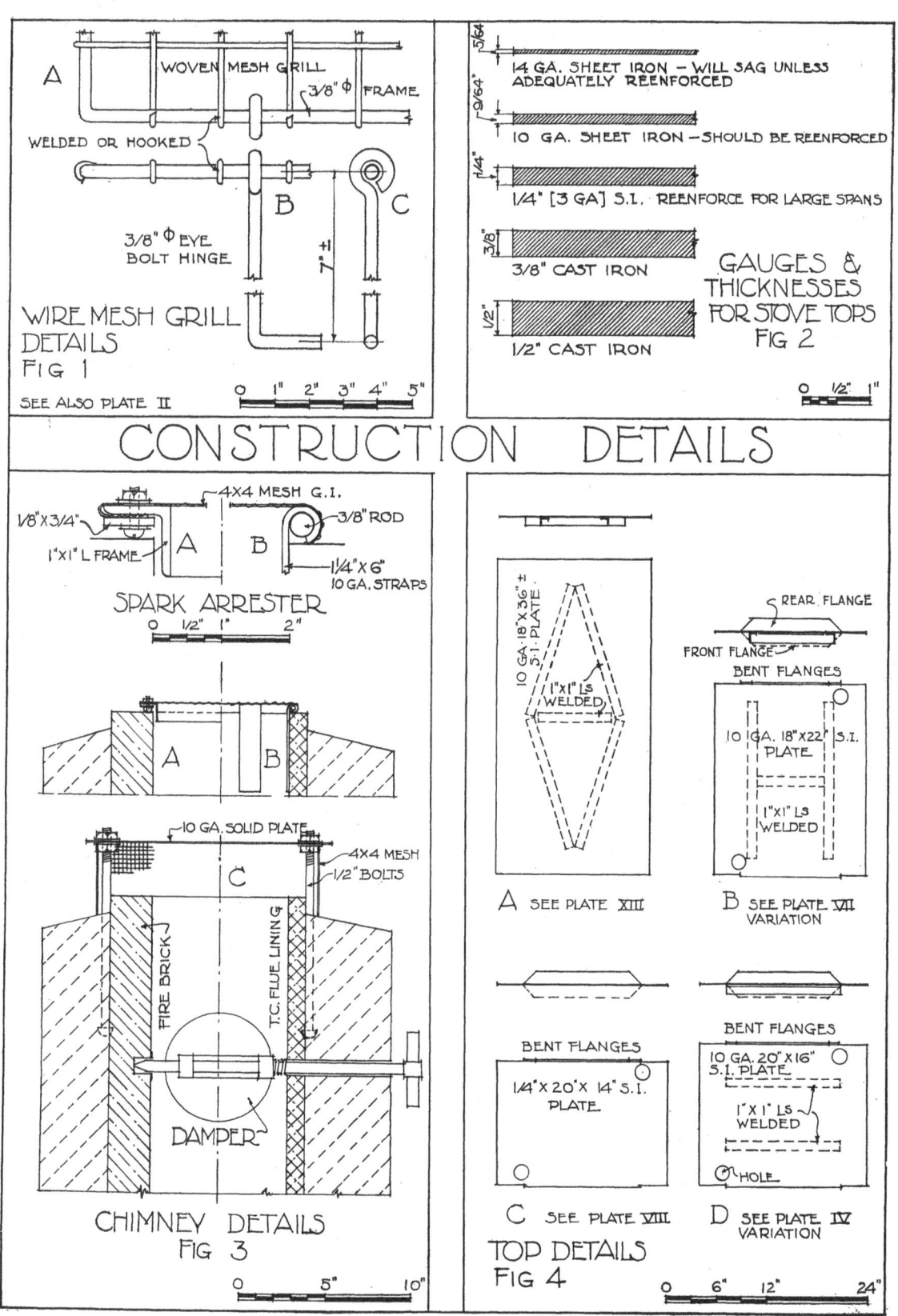

A WOVEN MESH GRILL
3/8"Φ FRAME
WELDED OR HOOKED
3/8"Φ EYE BOLT HINGE
B
C
7"±

WIRE MESH GRILL DETAILS
FIG 1
SEE ALSO PLATE II
0 1" 2" 3" 4" 5"

14 GA. SHEET IRON — WILL SAG UNLESS ADEQUATELY REENFORCED
5/64"
9/64"
10 GA. SHEET IRON — SHOULD BE REENFORCED
1/4"
1/4" [3 GA] S.I. REENFORCE FOR LARGE SPANS
3/8"
3/8" CAST IRON
1/2"
1/2" CAST IRON

GAUGES & THICKNESSES FOR STOVE TOPS
FIG 2
0 1/2" 1"

CONSTRUCTION DETAILS

4X4 MESH G.I.
1/8"X3/4"
3/8" ROD
1"X1" L FRAME
A
B
1/4"X6" 10 GA. STRAPS

SPARK ARRESTER
0 1/2" 1" 2"

A
B

10 GA. SOLID PLATE
4X4 MESH
1/2" BOLTS
C
FIRE BRICK
T.C. FLUE LINING
DAMPER

CHIMNEY DETAILS
FIG 3
0 5" 10"

10 GA. 18"X36"± S.I. PLATE
1"X1" LS WELDED

A SEE PLATE XIII

REAR FLANGE
FRONT FLANGE
BENT FLANGES
10 GA. 18"X22" S.I. PLATE
1"X1" LS WELDED

B SEE PLATE VII VARIATION

BENT FLANGES
1/4"X20"X14" S.I. PLATE

C SEE PLATE VIII

BENT FLANGES
10 GA. 20"X16" S.I. PLATE
1"X1" LS WELDED
HOLE

D SEE PLATE IV VARIATION

TOP DETAILS
FIG 4
0 6" 12" 24"

PLATE XXII

CONSTRUCTION DETAILS

COOKING STANDARD FOR CAMPFIRE USE

This cooking standard may be used either as a single standard (pl. XX, figs. 5 and 6) or as a double standard (pl. XXII–A, figs. 1 and 2). It is a simple unit of use primarily on picnic areas, and especially adapted for use by hunters and fishermen.

In this unit, facilities are provided for broiling on a grate, and for cooking otherwise on a plate or grate. Kettles may be hung on the hooks shown in figure 2.

This unit is generally installed with a small campfire circle. The provision for raising or lowering the irons on which the cooking is done, is shown in the details under figure 1.

The idea of the double standard shown in figure 2 originated in region 1 of the Forest Service.

CAST IRON AND SHEET IRON, STOVE DETAILS

The important requirements to be fulfilled in the design for the door on the front of the firebox are as follows:

(a) To construct the door of a quality of iron which will prevent the door from warping when exposed to heat.

(b) To make provisions so that the door may be securely closed.

(c) To provide a draft opening in the door.

(d) To provide hinges so that the door will remain hanging in its correct position.

The draft in the door as shown in figures 3, 4, and 5 may be through an opening which is constant (as in fig. 3), or it may be through holes, the area of which may be increased or decreased by a revolving lid (as in fig. 4), or by a sliding damper (as in fig. 5). If the type of draft opening shown in figure 3 is used, it seems advisable to install, in addition, a damper in the chimney to properly control the draft. The damper in the chimney is not generally required when there is provision for opening and closing the front draft as shown in figures 4 and 5.

Four methods of hinging the door at the front of the firebox are shown in figures 3, 4, 5, and 6. The method of attaching the doors with hinges as shown in figure 5 is the least desirable, and the methods shown in figures 3 and 4 are the most desirable. The kind of hinge shown in figure 5 does not always hold the door solidly in place.

Doors are also hinged at the top and at the bottom. The hinging of doors at the bottom should be discouraged, and the hinging of doors at the top does not seem to be as practical in actual use as hinging the doors on the side.

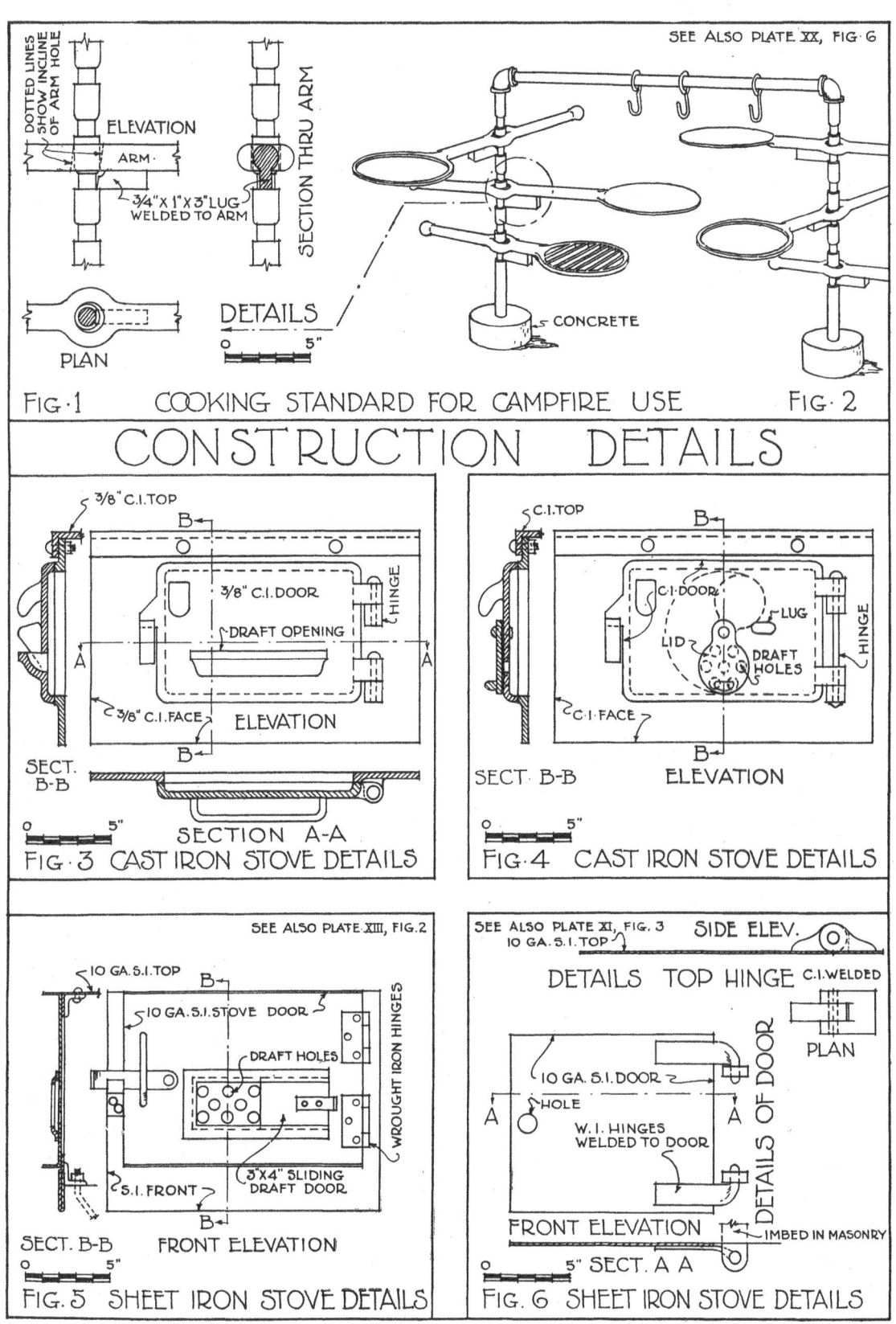

SEE ALSO PLATE XX, FIG·6

DOTTED LINES SHOW INCLINE OF ARM HOLE

ELEVATION

ARM·

SECTION THRU ARM

3/4"X 1"X 3" LUG WELDED TO ARM

PLAN

DETAILS

0 ——— 5"

CONCRETE

FIG·1   COOKING STANDARD FOR CAMPFIRE USE   FIG·2

CONSTRUCTION DETAILS

3/8" C.I. TOP

B

3/8" C.I. DOOR

HINGE

DRAFT OPENING

A   A

3/8" C.I. FACE

ELEVATION

B

SECT. B·B

0 — 5"

SECTION A-A

FIG·3 CAST IRON STOVE DETAILS

C.I. TOP

B

C.I. DOOR

LUG

LID

DRAFT HOLES

HINGE

C.I. FACE

SECT. B-B   ELEVATION

B

0 — 5"

FIG·4 CAST IRON STOVE DETAILS

SEE ALSO PLATE XIII, FIG.2

10 GA. S.I. TOP

B

10 GA. S.I. STOVE DOOR

DRAFT HOLES

WROUGHT IRON HINGES

3"X4" SLIDING DRAFT DOOR

S.I. FRONT

B

SECT. B-B   FRONT ELEVATION

0 — 5"

FIG·5 SHEET IRON STOVE DETAILS

SEE ALSO PLATE XI, FIG·3
10 GA. S.I. TOP

SIDE ELEV.

DETAILS TOP HINGE C.I. WELDED

PLAN

10 GA. S.I. DOOR

A   A

HOLE

W.I. HINGES WELDED TO DOOR

DETAILS OF DOOR

FRONT ELEVATION

IMBED IN MASONRY

0 — 5" SECT. A A

FIG·6 SHEET IRON STOVE DETAILS

PLATE XXII-A

FIREPLACE CONSTRUCTION
WITHIN SHELTERS

THE design of the fireplace to be constructed within a shelter must follow closely the fundamental requirements for the design of any interior fireplace. Ordinarily, the fireplace designed within a shelter building and primarily for use for warming purposes is higher and wider than the normal fireplace in the average residence.

The following are some of the important requirements which should be recognized in developing a proper design for such a fireplace.

GENERAL DESIGN

Any well-designed fireplace should have a proper draft which will eliminate any smoking.

The back of the fireplace should slope forward to the rear line of the throat as shown in the drawing. The maximum heat can be radiated into the room by splaying the sides.

The lining of the fireplace should be of fireclay brick, carefully laid in accordance with the directions contained on page 14.

THROAT AND FLUE

The most important detail of fireplace design concerns the throat and the flue, either or both of which, if not properly designed, cause failure in the practical use of the fireplace.

The horizontal net sectional area of the flue should be about one-twelfth to one-tenth of the area of the fireplace opening. The normal fireplace opening ranges from 2 feet 6 inches to 4 feet in width, 16 to 22 inches in depth, and 2 feet 6 inches to 3 feet in height. If the fireplace is abnormally high, then the area of the flue should be increased and may be as much as one-eighth of the area of the fireplace opening, in order to provide an adequate draft to properly remove the smoke.

In computing the area for the flue, care should be exercised to make certain that the net area is adopted. The sizes of the tile used for lining the flue are apt to be misleading in that round tile are designated by inside measurements and the rectangular or square tile are designated by outside measurements.

In the higher fireplaces with normal area of flue, all of the fire should be back of the rear line of the hood at the top of the fireplace. In reality, the damper in the fireplace constructed in shelter buildings can well be eliminated if the throat and flue are properly designed.

The throat should extend across the full width of the opening at the top of the fireplace and the front line of the throat should be as near the front of the fireplace as it is practical to make it. Its sectional area should be (when the damper is open) the same or very little less than that of the flue.

The flue must be reduced to its normal required size by sloping the sides as shown in the elevation, and the center of the flue must be directly over the middle of the fireplace. Any deflection which is to occur in the alinement of the flue must occur above this point where the flue reaches a normal and constant area. If the flue is deflected to one side immediately as it leaves the throat, one side of the fireplace will smoke.

The interior of the flue should not be plastered, as is sometimes done. This is not good construction because the plaster is apt to peel and break away from the brickwork, thus clogging the flue.

The down current of cold air which may occur when the fire is being started is overcome by the construction of a flat shelf. This shelf deflects the down-current of cool air and carries it back into the up-current of warm air. If this shelf is not constructed, there is a down draft at the back of the fireplace, especially when the fire is being started, thus driving smoke into the room. This down draft does not occur

FIREPLACE CONSTRUCTION

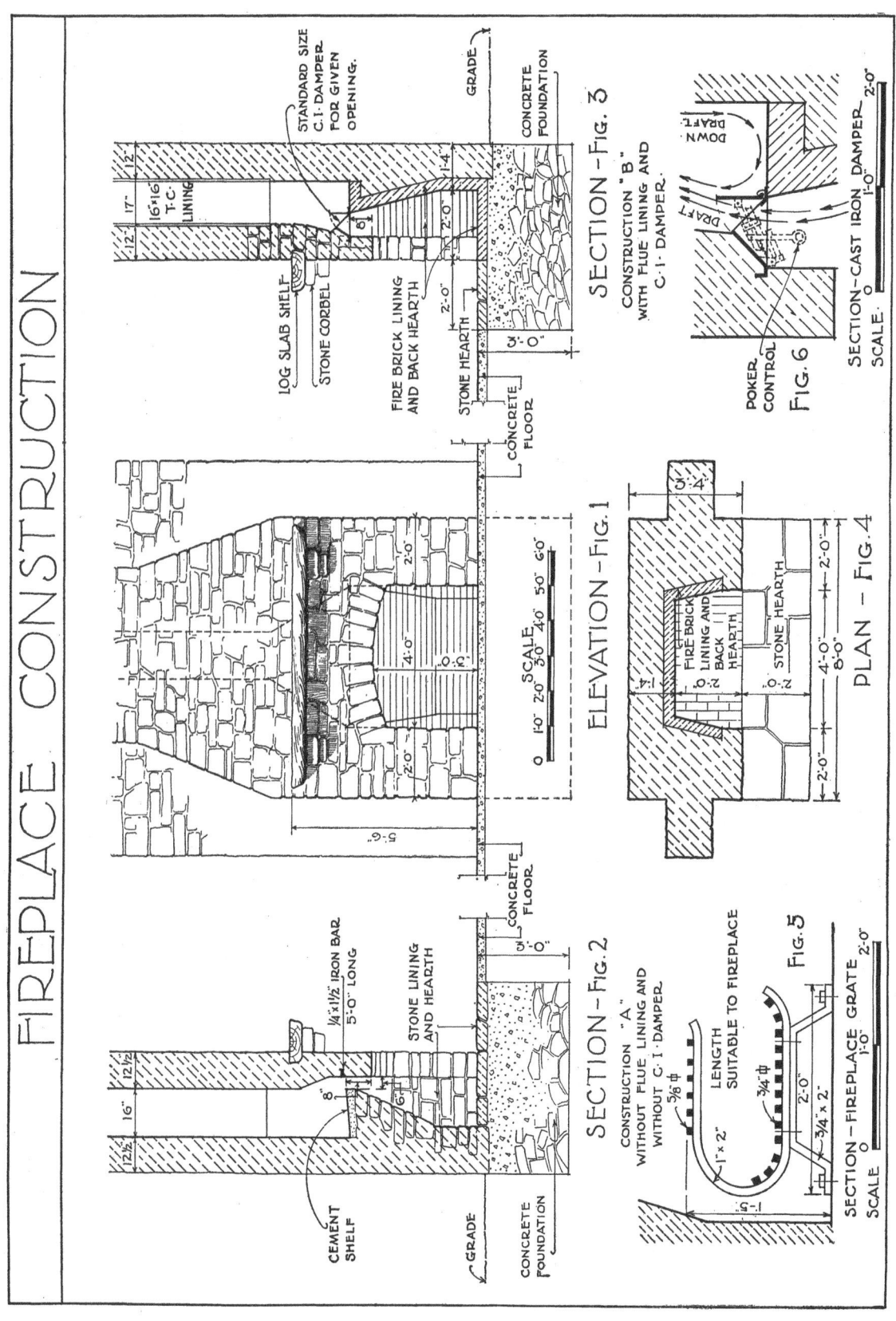

STANDARD SIZE C.I. DAMPER FOR GIVEN OPENING.

16"×16" T.C. LINING

12"   17"   12"

LOG SLAB SHELF

STONE CORBEL

FIRE BRICK LINING AND BACK HEARTH

STONE HEARTH

GRADE

CONCRETE FOUNDATION

2'-0"

CONCRETE FLOOR

0'-0"

3'-0"

SECTION – FIG. 3

CONSTRUCTION "B" WITH FLUE LINING AND C.I. DAMPER.

DOWN DRAFT

DRAFT

POKER CONTROL

FIG. 6

SECTION – CAST IRON DAMPER

SCALE 0   1'-0"   2'-0"

2'-0"

SCALE 0 1'-0" 2'-0" 3'-0" 4'-0" 5'-0" 6'-0"

4'-0"

2'-0"

5'-6"

CONCRETE FLOOR

0'-0"

ELEVATION – FIG. 1

0'-4"

FIRE BRICK LINING AND BACK HEARTH

STONE HEARTH

1'-4"

2'-0"

2'-0"   4'-0"   2'-0"

8'-0"

PLAN – FIG. 4

12½"   16"   12½"

12½"

8"

6"

CEMENT SHELF

¼"×1½" IRON BAR 5'-0" LONG

STONE LINING AND HEARTH

GRADE

CONCRETE FOUNDATION

2'-0"

CONCRETE FLOOR

0'-0"

SECTION – FIG. 2

CONSTRUCTION "A" WITHOUT FLUE LINING AND WITHOUT C.I. DAMPER.

5⁄8" ⏀

3⁄4" ⏀

LENGTH SUITABLE TO FIREPLACE

1"×2"

2'-0"

3⁄4"×2"

1'-5"

FIG. 5

SECTION – FIREPLACE GRATE

SCALE 0   1'-0"   2'-0"

PLATE XXIII

81

after the fire is well started and the flue is sufficiently heated so that the entire air current is upward. The smoke shelf might be sloped slightly, in order that if any rain comes down the chimney during heavy storms this moisture would drain into the fireplace.

In many fireplaces, a damper is desirable. This damper should be installed as shown in the detail and must open through the full length of the throat. The damper in the throat of the fireplace is really only necessary in order to close the fireplace during the period of the year when the fireplace is not in use, and thus protect the interior of the building against any drafts of cool air, insects, etc., which might come through the chimney.

The flue is usually lined with terra cotta in preference to any other construction.

GOOD AND BAD STONEWORK

THE stonework in a great many of the existing fireplaces which have been observed by the author is not well done. The type of stonework which seems appropriate and inappropriate for camp stoves and fireplaces is illustrated on the accompanying plates (XXIV and XXV).

The mistakes which are frequently made in the texture of stonework in fireplaces are the following:

A. Using a type of stone which is not adapted for this kind of a unit, as shown in plate XXIV, figure 6, and in plate XXV, figure 6.

B. Laying the stonework on an unnatural bed which does not create a pleasing composition in the camp stove or fireplace design (pl. XXIV, fig. 2; pl. XXV, fig. 6).

C. Using a type of texture which is too formal for such a feature in naturalistic surroundings (pl. XXV, fig. 4).

D. Using cobblestones which are not carefully laid and produce a loose and unstable effect (pl. XXIV, fig. 4).

It is very essential that the stonework be constructed in a permanent way and that the texture of the stonework be appropriate to the naturalistic surroundings.

So far as is practical, the horizontal effect which is excellently illustrated in plate XXV, figures 3 and 5, and plate XXIV, figure 3, should be procured if possible.

No camp stove or fireplace should be constructed to present the formal effect of stone texture which is illustrated in plate XXV, figure 4. The use of broken stone with sharp angles and laid in such a manner that the surface texture is very uneven and the mortar joints deep, as shown in plate XXV, figure 6, should also be very definitely avoided. This same type of stone, if carefully selected and well laid, can produce an appropriate and desirable effect. When laid as shown in plate XXV, figure 6, it gives the effect of an uninteresting pile of stones with no character in texture.

The stone which is laid on an unnatural bed, as shown in plate XXIV, figure 2, and producing the vertical effect, increases the apparent height of the camp stove; while the stone laid on a natural bed and producing a horizontal effect, as shown in plate XXIV, figure 3, decreases the apparent height of the camp stove.

The camp stove which is constructed of oversized units of stone with rough surface, as shown in plate XXIV, figure 6, is to be discouraged.

In general, it is not a logical procedure to use in every instance the stone which is available in any specific locality without making an effort to find stone which is better adapted for camp stove construction.

The above discussion relates primarily to stoves and fireplaces that expose a surface of stonework sufficient to be designated as a "wall." In the case of the primitive and naturalistic fireplaces, both the size of the stones and the method of laying may be varied as shown in the various drawings.

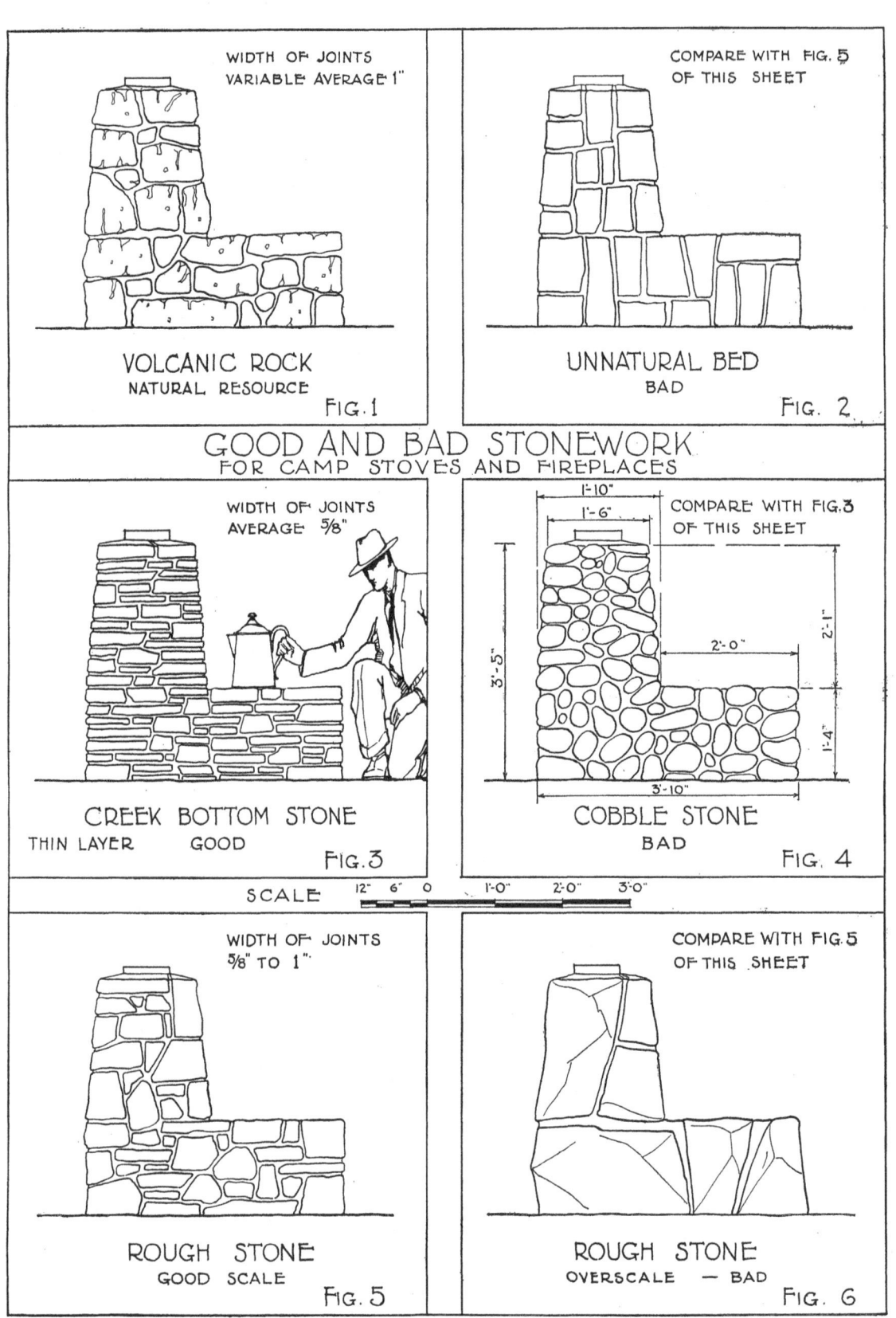

WIDTH OF JOINTS
VARIABLE AVERAGE 1"

VOLCANIC ROCK
NATURAL RESOURCE
FIG. 1

COMPARE WITH FIG. 5
OF THIS SHEET

UNNATURAL BED
BAD
FIG. 2

GOOD AND BAD STONEWORK
FOR CAMP STOVES AND FIREPLACES

WIDTH OF JOINTS
AVERAGE 5/8"

CREEK BOTTOM STONE
THIN LAYER   GOOD
FIG. 3

COMPARE WITH FIG. 3
OF THIS SHEET

COBBLE STONE
BAD
FIG. 4

SCALE   12" 6" 0   1'-0" 2'-0" 3'-0"

WIDTH OF JOINTS
5/8" TO 1"

ROUGH STONE
GOOD SCALE
FIG. 5

COMPARE WITH FIG. 5
OF THIS SHEET

ROUGH STONE
OVERSCALE — BAD
FIG. 6

PLATE XXIV

84

WIDTH OF JOINTS
⅝" TO 1"

TRIMMED STONE AT RANDOM
GOOD
FIG. 1

COMPARE WITH FIG. 3
OF THIS SHEET.

LOOSE RUBBLE
BAD
FIG. 2

GOOD AND BAD STONEWORK
FOR CAMP STOVES AND FIREPLACES

WIDTH OF JOINTS
AVERAGE ⅝"

CREEK BOTTOM STONE
COURSE   GOOD
FIG. 3

COMPARE WITH FIG.1
OF THIS SHEET.

1'-10"
1'-6"
2'-0"
3'-5"
2'-1"
1'-4"
3'-10"

STONE BLOCK
BAD FOR NATURAL SETTING
FIG. 4

SCALE   12" 6" 0   1'-0"   2'-0"   3'-0"

WIDTH OF JOINTS
½" TO ¾"

SPLIT STONE
GOOD
FIG 5

COMPARE WITH FIG. 5
OF THIS SHEET.

PILED STONE
BAD
FIG. 6

PLATE XXV

UNDESIRABLE TYPES

FIGURE 1

A fireplace unit, whether portable or stationary, with walls of concrete, is out of place in any natural surrounding. The concrete fails to weather sufficiently to produce any softening effect and it disintegrates under extreme changes of temperature (especially when doused with water).

FIGURE 2

The hard and formal cut stone or dimension stone should not be used in any natural setting. Such fireplaces (well designed) may have their proper place on some parts of private estates and home grounds; but not in the forest. An equally undesirable type of design is that which exposes the fire-clay brick across the front of the fireplace, as shown in figure 2. The use of large grate bars, spaced so far apart that the grill is not practical for cooking purposes, should be avoided.

FIGURE 3

As stated elsewhere in this discussion, the standard grate, without sides as shown in this sketch, is only practical and desirable on picnic areas which are intensively used, and where the fire hazard is negligible. There is a proper use for this grate, as shown in plate I, figures 4, 6B, and 6C, and in plates III and III–A.

FIGURE 4

An example of a "clumsy" fireplace, with an unusually large fire box and a type of cobblestone texture which makes this feature exceedingly undesirable.

FIGURE 5

The stonework in such fireplaces is very "cold" and unattractive. The firebox has no fire-clay brick lining. The use of the lower grate is not practical and the solid attachment of the grate or the bars to the stone masonry causes undue damage because of expansion from the heat.

FIGURE 6

This type is all chimney and no fireplace. It has all of the undesirable qualities which could possibly be introduced into a single unit. It is more of an ill-proportioned chimney than a fireplace.

FIGURE 7

An incongruous type of construction, with a brick chimney and stone masonry sides, where the stone texture is extremely unattractive because of the regular courses of small boulders, which create an unstable effect.

FIGURE 8

A monumental type of fireplace which would "roast an ox" as quickly as it would broil lamb chops. The top of the firebox (approximately 36 to 40 inches in height) is too high. The stonework is much too fine in texture and the entire massive effect is one which should be avoided.

FIGURES 9, 10, AND 11

The "ice box" and the "oil drum" types are to be avoided on every possible occasion because of their very inappropriate design.

FORMAL TYPE
BARS OVERSPACED

CONCRETE BLOCK
FIG 1

SIMPLE GRATE
WITHOUT SIDES

FIG. 2

FIG. 3

RUBBLE MASONRY
POOR DESIGN AND EXECUTION

FIG.4

UNDESIRABLE TYPES

ASHLAR BLOCK
DOUBLE GRATE
FIG. 5

THE "STONE PILE"
FIG. 6

RUBBLE
AND BRICK
FIG. 7

"MAUSOLEUM"
FIG. 8

"ICE-BOX"
ON RUBBLE
FIG. 9

"OIL DRUM"-FIG. 10

"ICE BOX"
ON CONCRETE
FIG. 11

PLATE XXVI

FREQUENT MISTAKES

IN FIREPLACE AND CAMP STOVE
DESIGN AND CONSTRUCTION

A. Structures too large and too conspicuous to be in harmony with surroundings.

B. Structures too complicated in design and construction.

C. Lack of proper setting, or necessary screening, as viewed from important points.

D. Lack of character in texture of stonework and unfortunate selection of stones.

E. Lack of consideration for correct details of construction in lining walls or firebox.

F. Use of common mortar for fire-clay brick lining and making joints in fire-clay brick construction too thick.

G. Excessive size of firebox.

H. Incorrect construction in attaching bars and top plates to masonry without making provision for expansion.

I. Spacing of bars in top grate too far apart.

J. Incorrect reenforcing and lack of proper attachment for top plate, in order to prevent warping.

K. Having top plate too thick and thus preventing efficient heating.

L. Existence of sharp corners in construction of stone masonry.

M. Making stone masonry walls so thick that there is inconvenience in using the top plate for cooking.

N. Lack of provision for adequate flat wall space on which to set cooking utensils.

O. Building chimneys with flues on fireplaces which do not have a solid top plate. In such instances the flue is useless.

P. Using too many movable parts and of not sufficient strength to prevent them from being easily bent or broken.

CAMP UNIT LAYOUTS

No DISCUSSION with reference to camp stoves and fireplaces can be complete without including information with reference to the lay-out, especially of camp units.

In the picnic area a tent or shelter is very seldom used. The area in which the family automobile may be parked is usually in a parking space which is within a reasonable distance of the picnic table and fireplace. Food and other supplies are taken from the automobile, in its parking space, to the picnic table. The picnickers prepare, to the extent necessary, the food which must be cooked generally over a fireplace.

In the camp area a tent or shelter is almost always used and the camp stove is the generally acceptable cooking unit. The automobile must be parked very close to the camp unit because it is continuously in use as the family larder to which access must be procured before and after each of the three daily meals. A separate general parking area removed from the camp units is not a practicable solution to the problem.

The solving of the design for the camp unit is more of a problem than the picnic area unit involving only the table and fireplace.

The camp unit may be occupied by the automobile alone, or by an automobile with a trailer. The trailer presents a problem which is different from the problem when only the automobile is used.

The two sketches "A" and "B" indicate two of the methods for developing the camp unit in connection with the trailer. The more practical method of providing space for the automobile and trailer is that of developing a loop, as shown in sketch "B." This loop, when meeting the requirements of a single camp unit, may be a one-way narrow drive, or only of sufficient width to provide for the automobile and trailer, or where the loop meets the requirements of two or more camp units the roadway should be "two-way."

It may be desirable in some locations, where a loop is not practicable, to use a spur in which to back the automobile and trailer, as shown in sketch "A." There may be other camp units in which it is desirable to provide for one or more families in a single parking space adjacent to the camp unit, as shown in sketch "C."

The sketches marked "D" to "O", inclusive, show the possibilities for the arrangement of the camp unit in order to provide for the automobile, tent, camp stove (and where desired, campfire) and the picnic table. In some areas, a warming-fire may not be required, and therefore only a camp stove is used, as shown in sketches "F", "H", "J", and "N." In other locations, it is desirable to provide a convertible type of camp stove, which may meet the requirements for cooking and for a warming-fire, as shown in plates X and XI.

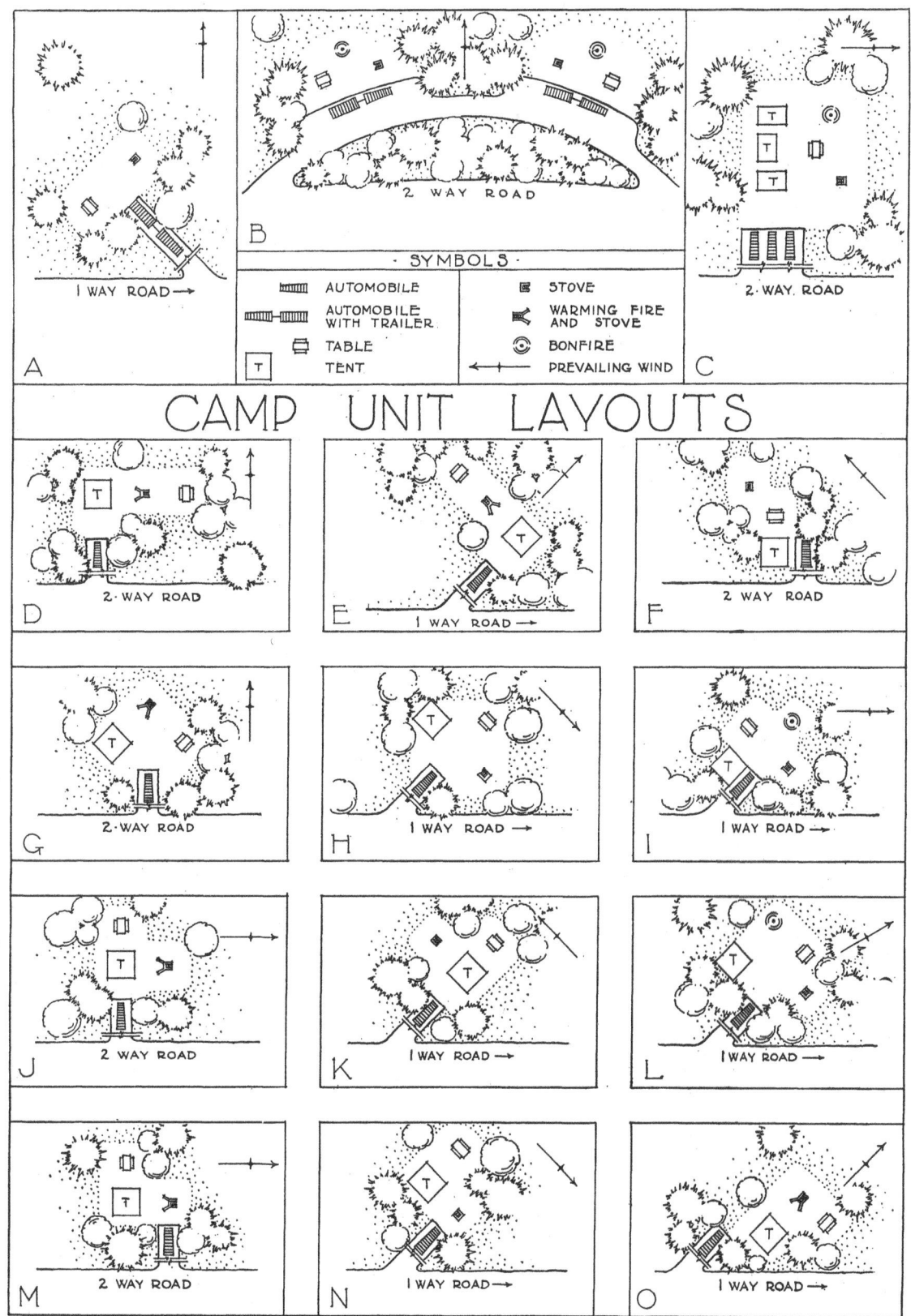

CAMP UNIT LAYOUTS

SYMBOLS

AUTOMOBILE		STOVE	
AUTOMOBILE WITH TRAILER		WARMING FIRE AND STOVE	
TABLE		BONFIRE	
T TENT		PREVAILING WIND	

A — 1 WAY ROAD →

B — 2 WAY ROAD

C — 2 WAY ROAD

D — 2 WAY ROAD

E — 1 WAY ROAD →

F — 2 WAY ROAD

G — 2 WAY ROAD

H — 1 WAY ROAD →

I — 1 WAY ROAD →

J — 2 WAY ROAD

K — 1 WAY ROAD →

L — 1 WAY ROAD →

M — 2 WAY ROAD

N — 1 WAY ROAD →

O — 1 WAY ROAD →

PLATE XXVII

80796°—37

A CATALOG OF SELECTED
DOVER BOOKS
IN ALL FIELDS OF INTEREST

A CATALOG OF SELECTED DOVER
BOOKS IN ALL FIELDS OF INTEREST

100 BEST-LOVED POEMS, Edited by Philip Smith. "The Passionate Shepherd to His Love," "Shall I compare thee to a summer's day?" "Death, be not proud," "The Raven," "The Road Not Taken," plus works by Blake, Wordsworth, Byron, Shelley, Keats, many others. 96pp. 5³⁄₁₆ x 8¼. 0-486-28553-7

100 SMALL HOUSES OF THE THIRTIES, Brown-Blodgett Company. Exterior photographs and floor plans for 100 charming structures. Illustrations of models accompanied by descriptions of interiors, color schemes, closet space, and other amenities. 200 illustrations. 112pp. 8⅜ x 11. 0-486-44131-8

1000 TURN-OF-THE-CENTURY HOUSES: With Illustrations and Floor Plans, Herbert C. Chivers. Reproduced from a rare edition, this showcase of homes ranges from cottages and bungalows to sprawling mansions. Each house is meticulously illustrated and accompanied by complete floor plans. 256pp. 9⅜ x 12¼.
0-486-45596-3

101 GREAT AMERICAN POEMS, Edited by The American Poetry & Literacy Project. Rich treasury of verse from the 19th and 20th centuries includes works by Edgar Allan Poe, Robert Frost, Walt Whitman, Langston Hughes, Emily Dickinson, T. S. Eliot, other notables. 96pp. 5³⁄₁₆ x 8¼. 0-486-40158-8

101 GREAT SAMURAI PRINTS, Utagawa Kuniyoshi. Kuniyoshi was a master of the warrior woodblock print — and these 18th-century illustrations represent the pinnacle of his craft. Full-color portraits of renowned Japanese samurais pulse with movement, passion, and remarkably fine detail. 112pp. 8⅜ x 11. 0-486-46523-3

ABC OF BALLET, Janet Grosser. Clearly worded, abundantly illustrated little guide defines basic ballet-related terms: arabesque, battement, pas de chat, relevé, sissonne, many others. Pronunciation guide included. Excellent primer. 48pp. 4³⁄₁₆ x 5¾.
0-486-40871-X

ACCESSORIES OF DRESS: An Illustrated Encyclopedia, Katherine Lester and Bess Viola Oerke. Illustrations of hats, veils, wigs, cravats, shawls, shoes, gloves, and other accessories enhance an engaging commentary that reveals the humor and charm of the many-sided story of accessorized apparel. 644 figures and 59 plates. 608pp. 6 ⅛ x 9¼.
0-486-43378-1

ADVENTURES OF HUCKLEBERRY FINN, Mark Twain. Join Huck and Jim as their boyhood adventures along the Mississippi River lead them into a world of excitement, danger, and self-discovery. Humorous narrative, lyrical descriptions of the Mississippi valley, and memorable characters. 224pp. 5³⁄₁₆ x 8¼. 0-486-28061-6

ALICE STARMORE'S BOOK OF FAIR ISLE KNITTING, Alice Starmore. A noted designer from the region of Scotland's Fair Isle explores the history and techniques of this distinctive, stranded-color knitting style and provides copious illustrated instructions for 14 original knitwear designs. 208pp. 8⅜ x 10⅞. 0-486-47218-3

ALICE'S ADVENTURES IN WONDERLAND, Lewis Carroll. Beloved classic about a little girl lost in a topsy-turvy land and her encounters with the White Rabbit, March Hare, Mad Hatter, Cheshire Cat, and other delightfully improbable characters. 42 illustrations by Sir John Tenniel. 96pp. 5³⁄₁₆ x 8¼. 0-486-27543-4

AMERICA'S LIGHTHOUSES: An Illustrated History, Francis Ross Holland. Profusely illustrated fact-filled survey of American lighthouses since 1716. Over 200 stations — East, Gulf, and West coasts, Great Lakes, Hawaii, Alaska, Puerto Rico, the Virgin Islands, and the Mississippi and St. Lawrence Rivers. 240pp. 8 x 10¾.
0-486-25576-X

AN ENCYCLOPEDIA OF THE VIOLIN, Alberto Bachmann. Translated by Frederick H. Martens. Introduction by Eugene Ysaye. First published in 1925, this renowned reference remains unsurpassed as a source of essential information, from construction and evolution to repertoire and technique. Includes a glossary and 73 illustrations. 496pp. 6⅛ x 9¼. 0-486-46618-3

ANIMALS: 1,419 Copyright-Free Illustrations of Mammals, Birds, Fish, Insects, etc., Selected by Jim Harter. Selected for its visual impact and ease of use, this outstanding collection of wood engravings presents over 1,000 species of animals in extremely lifelike poses. Includes mammals, birds, reptiles, amphibians, fish, insects, and other invertebrates. 284pp. 9 x 12. 0-486-23766-4

THE ANNALS, Tacitus. Translated by Alfred John Church and William Jackson Brodribb. This vital chronicle of Imperial Rome, written by the era's great historian, spans A.D. 14-68 and paints incisive psychological portraits of major figures, from Tiberius to Nero. 416pp. 5³⁄₁₆ x 8¼. 0-486-45236-0

ANTIGONE, Sophocles. Filled with passionate speeches and sensitive probing of moral and philosophical issues, this powerful and often-performed Greek drama reveals the grim fate that befalls the children of Oedipus. Footnotes. 64pp. 5³⁄₁₆ x 8 ¼. 0-486-27804-2

ART DECO DECORATIVE PATTERNS IN FULL COLOR, Christian Stoll. Reprinted from a rare 1910 portfolio, 160 sensuous and exotic images depict a breathtaking array of florals, geometrics, and abstracts — all elegant in their stark simplicity. 64pp. 8⅜ x 11. 0-486-44862-2

THE ARTHUR RACKHAM TREASURY: 86 Full-Color Illustrations, Arthur Rackham. Selected and Edited by Jeff A. Menges. A stunning treasury of 86 full-page plates span the famed English artist's career, from *Rip Van Winkle* (1905) to masterworks such as *Undine, A Midsummer Night's Dream,* and *Wind in the Willows* (1939). 96pp. 8⅜ x 11.
0-486-44685-9

THE AUTHENTIC GILBERT & SULLIVAN SONGBOOK, W. S. Gilbert and A. S. Sullivan. The most comprehensive collection available, this songbook includes selections from every one of Gilbert and Sullivan's light operas. Ninety-two numbers are presented uncut and unedited, and in their original keys. 410pp. 9 x 12.
0-486-23482-7

THE AWAKENING, Kate Chopin. First published in 1899, this controversial novel of a New Orleans wife's search for love outside a stifling marriage shocked readers. Today, it remains a first-rate narrative with superb characterization. New introductory Note. 128pp. 5³⁄₁₆ x 8¼. 0-486-27786-0

BASIC DRAWING, Louis Priscilla. Beginning with perspective, this commonsense manual progresses to the figure in movement, light and shade, anatomy, drapery, composition, trees and landscape, and outdoor sketching. Black-and-white illustrations throughout. 128pp. 8⅜ x 11. 0-486-45815-6

Browse over 9,000 books at www.doverpublications.com

THE BATTLES THAT CHANGED HISTORY, Fletcher Pratt. Historian profiles 16 crucial conflicts, ancient to modern, that changed the course of Western civilization. Gripping accounts of battles led by Alexander the Great, Joan of Arc, Ulysses S. Grant, other commanders. 27 maps. 352pp. 5⅜ x 8½.   0-486-41129-X

BEETHOVEN'S LETTERS, Ludwig van Beethoven. Edited by Dr. A. C. Kalischer. Features 457 letters to fellow musicians, friends, greats, patrons, and literary men. Reveals musical thoughts, quirks of personality, insights, and daily events. Includes 15 plates. 410pp. 5⅜ x 8½.   0-486-22769-3

BERNICE BOBS HER HAIR AND OTHER STORIES, F. Scott Fitzgerald. This brilliant anthology includes 6 of Fitzgerald's most popular stories: "The Diamond as Big as the Ritz," the title tale, "The Offshore Pirate," "The Ice Palace," "The Jelly Bean," and "May Day." 176pp. 5⅜ x 8½.   0-486-47049-0

BESLER'S BOOK OF FLOWERS AND PLANTS: 73 Full-Color Plates from Hortus Eystettensis, 1613, Basilius Besler. Here is a selection of magnificent plates from the *Hortus Eystettensis,* which vividly illustrated and identified the plants, flowers, and trees that thrived in the legendary German garden at Eichstätt. 80pp. 8⅜ x 11.
0-486-46005-3

THE BOOK OF KELLS, Edited by Blanche Cirker. Painstakingly reproduced from a rare facsimile edition, this volume contains full-page decorations, portraits, illustrations, plus a sampling of textual leaves with exquisite calligraphy and ornamentation. 32 full-color illustrations. 32pp. 9⅜ x 12¼.   0-486-24345-1

THE BOOK OF THE CROSSBOW: With an Additional Section on Catapults and Other Siege Engines, Ralph Payne-Gallwey. Fascinating study traces history and use of crossbow as military and sporting weapon, from Middle Ages to modern times. Also covers related weapons: balistas, catapults, Turkish bows, more. Over 240 illustrations. 400pp. 7¼ x 10⅛.   0-486-28720-3

THE BUNGALOW BOOK: Floor Plans and Photos of 112 Houses, 1910, Henry L. Wilson. Here are 112 of the most popular and economic blueprints of the early 20th century — plus an illustration or photograph of each completed house. A wonderful time capsule that still offers a wealth of valuable insights. 160pp. 8⅜ x 11.
0-486-45104-6

THE CALL OF THE WILD, Jack London. A classic novel of adventure, drawn from London's own experiences as a Klondike adventurer, relating the story of a heroic dog caught in the brutal life of the Alaska Gold Rush. Note. 64pp. 5³⁄₁₆ x 8¼.
0-486-26472-6

CANDIDE, Voltaire. Edited by Francois-Marie Arouet. One of the world's great satires since its first publication in 1759. Witty, caustic skewering of romance, science, philosophy, religion, government — nearly all human ideals and institutions. 112pp. 5³⁄₁₆ x 8¼.   0-486-26689-3

CELEBRATED IN THEIR TIME: Photographic Portraits from the George Grantham Bain Collection, Edited by Amy Pastan. With an Introduction by Michael Carlebach. Remarkable portrait gallery features 112 rare images of Albert Einstein, Charlie Chaplin, the Wright Brothers, Henry Ford, and other luminaries from the worlds of politics, art, entertainment, and industry. 128pp. 8⅜ x 11.   0-486-46754-6

CHARIOTS FOR APOLLO: The NASA History of Manned Lunar Spacecraft to 1969, Courtney G. Brooks, James M. Grimwood, and Loyd S. Swenson, Jr. This illustrated history by a trio of experts is the definitive reference on the Apollo spacecraft and lunar modules. It traces the vehicles' design, development, and operation in space. More than 100 photographs and illustrations. 576pp. 6¾ x 9¼.   0-486-46756-2

Browse over 9,000 books at www.doverpublications.com